STRIKE THE TENTS

The Story of the Chautauqua

By

CHARLES F. HORNER

Author of

The Life of James Redpath
The Speaker and the Audience
The Road that Leads . . .

DORRANCE & COMPANY
PHILADELPHIA

781.1
HR

LC
6301
C°5
H6

To

CRAWFORD A. PEFFER

AND

HARRY P. HARRISON

AND TO THE MEMORY OF

KEITH VAWTER

AND

VERNON HARRISON

CONTENTS

STRIKE THE TENTS

THE STORY OF THE CHAUTAUQUA

THE SOIL WAS FERTILE

The lives of three Horner men, Grandfather Joel, Father William and I, Charles, have spanned more than all the years of the life of this Republic.

The history on the maternal side is similar. Mother's father, James Barron, was born a few months after George Washington became President. Mother lived to a good old age and I, by the Grace of God, live happily in an America which my forbears could not have envisaged, and which I cannot quite comprehend as a reality.

The story of my life, which seems to be but a flash from the perils and the joys of storm and fire on the open prairie, to the bewildering movement of today, may scarcely merit the printing in a book. Yet the kind of life it was, the scenes in it, the character of the people who crossed its trail or traveled part of the way with me, the riches here, the poverty there, the hope, the ambition, the liberty, and, may I say modestly, the self reliance in it, all are of an America which I can never find again. No doubt I live in a greater America today, but of its flaming effulgence or of its occasional sickening despair, I have no adequate concept.

Without any thought of compiling an autobiography, I sketch a few incidents and facts in my early life, because the way I lived, the hope that loomed high in my mind, the physical hardship that I endured, and the stern realization that if I would acquire or achieve anything of worth, I must expect both without aid; those things were of the common experience of the people I knew so many years ago. That experience is of the essence of an Americanism in the days gone by and it found expression in the Chautauqua movement that swept the country in the first three decades of this century.

My grandfather, Joel Horner, was a good type of American pioneer. He was born in Trenton, New Jersey, in 1788, the year before George Washington became president. His wife died when their two sons were just reaching manhood. The lads soon left for the Far West, leaving Joel alone. In 1837 he yielded to the lure of the West and traveled by team through Pennsylvania. When he reached the Ohio River he built a raft, upon which he loaded his possessions, and floated downstream until he reached Indiana. He abandoned his raft and rolled onward in his lumbering wagon drawn by sad-eyed oxen. He explored Indiana and Illinois, pausing here to look around and there to get a job. Wisconsin was his goal, but his journey stretched through two years before he finally arrived. Chicago wasn't much of a town and Milwaukee was a village that had been organized only two or three years. He felled trees on what became the site of some of Milwaukee's finest buildings.

Joel found land sixteen miles from Milwaukee and acquired title to it. His acres were covered by a dense forest, which he finally cleared. There were weeks at a time when he never saw a white face, although he saw many Indians who never did him any harm. After a few years he found and married a dark-eyed Irish immigrant named Bridget Curran, who was my grandmother. Her people, the Kelleys, the Coons, the Daileys and the Burns, were numerous around Milwaukee and Racine.

Joel and Bridget had four sons. My father, William, was born in 1847. When he was seventeen and lacked seven inches of the stature he afterwards attained, he enlisted in the Union Army, and found himself on the battle line within sixty days. Not much time for training for him, and he didn't need much because the lads of the neighborhood had been drilling and marching for many weeks. Besides, with a rifle, he could pick a squirrel from a tree and, occasionally, a bird from the air. Although he was in service only the last year of the Civil War, he participated in five important battles.

Returning to Wisconsin, he acquired a farm in Dunn County. The land was covered with trees and brush, and he cleared it with his own hands. He bought and sold stock, raised some crops and spent some of his winters in the lumber camps to get cash for his operations.

James Barron was born in Dublin, Ireland, in 1789. Twenty-odd years afterwards he sailed for Philadelphia with his young wife, but she died and was buried at sea. Later, he married a bright Irish girl named Mary Alice Leigh, an immigrant from County Meath. The two pushed out into Wisconsin and settled in Dunn

County, where most of their neighbors were Indians. James Barron, for all his adventurous spirit, was a recluse. He was always surrounded with books and spent the latter years of his life in meditation. He and Mary Alice had eight sons, all six-footers, and one daughter, Martha Barron, my mother. She was a very beautiful girl, and William Horner fell in love with her at once. They were married when she was sixteen. I am their third child and only son.

William Horner was a giant in strength. He labored with his muscles as no other man I ever saw. He could strip from his body the filth of soil and stockyards, dress himself in white linen and broadcloth and drive good horses with pride. He surrounded himself with books, and in the dim light of an oil lamp at night he memorized page after page which he would repeat as he went about his work.

Martha Horner almost literally danced her way through the drudgery of my boyhood days. Through all her toil she moved with the grace of tall lilies bending in the breeze. There was always a song on her lips and her voice was like a lark.

We moved to Nebraska in 1886, when I was eight years old. My father erected good buildings on his ranch near the old town of Plum Creek, in the Platte Valley. The country was young and most of its soil had not been disturbed by the plow. The prairies, boundless and beautiful, stretched in level lustre to the east and the west until their encircling vastness was merged into the horizon. To the north and south, miles away, the grassy expanse lost itself in the viridity of low hills that skirted the valley.   It was a land of bare beauty and a place for dreams, but it held hidden terrors which, all too often, raged across the endless plains.

We were scarcely settled in our new and wonderful home before a prairie fire scourged the valley for miles. In the charred waste of our acres, only our house remained.   Our barns, our equipment and some of our stock were consumed.

We survived that and learned to meet fiery rage with cunning.   We lived through the historical blizzards of 1888, when with all my nine-year-old strength I helped my father drag freezing people from the fury of the storm into the living warmth of our ranch home.

Through spring, summer and fall, day in and day out, until I was fourteen, I rode herd on the open range.   I suffered the pangs of heat and thirst and weariness, but there was ample reward in the expansive feeling the far-flung plains conferred.   The vista was boundless and my vision was limited only by my capacity to think.

The old Mormon trail stretched across our grazing land.   The ruts of the old road were still deep although grass grew over the tracks made by the unnumbered thousands of covered wagons and laboring teams of oxen and horses and mules.   My imagination was as free as the fleet legs of my horse as we galloped along the worn road.   In fancy, I beheld the mighty empire in the West built by the survivors of the tens of thousands of sweating pioneers who struggled and prayed and swore and fought their course along the old highway.

The days were long and hot and sometimes wet. My food was the lunch I carried in my saddlebag. The canteen of water was usually dry long before the day was spent and I had to suffer from thirst or drink the bitter alkaline water from buffalo wallows. When the bellies of the herd were filled and the animals were content to rest, there was ample time for thought and for books. My father's example was always before me. Out there on the prairie I read Barnes' *History of the United States,* Townsend's *Civil Government,* the Declaration of Independence and the Constitution, until I could recite them from first to last. I was not particularly bright, but there was nothing else to do. I lived in a Union Soldier community where the Government of the United States and a devout patriotism for America were of the fabric of speech and ideals. At least it was that way around our house.

After our disastrous fire, although we had been in Nebraska less than six months, the kind settlers, for miles around, raised a sizable fund of cash among themselves and offered it to my father. Many of them could ill afford the money they gave, but their action was characteristic of men who had had much trouble of their own. Father refused to accept their bounty, but he was deeply touched by their generosity.

When drought, blizzards and low prices scourged the valley, goodhearted people from afar sent seed, coal, clothing and cash to our community. Father, like many others of his kind, would have none of the kindly charity. He scoffed at the idea of applying for a pension for many years. It seems that he was entitled to it, but he held that his debt to the country was greater than any obligation the Government owed to him.

During the winter months I attended our country school. It was a good one with an admirable teacher. It was two miles away, but my sisters and I thought nothing of walking to it and back again each day. Father was director of the school board, a position he held in the various places where he lived for nearly forty years.

When I was thirteen years old Father placed me in high school in Lexington, Nebraska, the old cow town which has become quite a little city. It was the same Plum Creek of earlier days. There again he was promptly elected as director of the school board. It was the first regular schooling I had, although on Saturdays, Sundays and during vacation it was always back to the herds for me.

Due to Father's urging for hard work, and to the genius of the superintendent of schools who gave me much tutoring, I managed to graduate when I was fifteen years old. That was in 1894. I was successful in passing an examination and received a teacher's certificate. Then came the most devastating drought in the history of the valley. Day after day a yellow sun spat its malicious fire onto the land. The grass curled under the blasts, and farmers, their leathery faces blistered anew, watched their crops die. There was little to do because the crops were gone and the cattle could roam almost at will. Every day that I could be spared I rode far and wide looking for a school to teach. My grades were high in the nineties and I carried warm letters of praise from important men. School-board men looked at them with approval but regarded my lank frame with doubt. Inevitably came the killing question "How old are you?" They were kind and explained that there would be many pupils older than I and that I was far too young. Finally, the last day before school was due to start I was engaged. I think all the other teachers didn't care for the place I found. At any rate, I was a teacher at thirty dollars a month. I taught in a sod schoolhouse and lived two miles away in a dugout. The place was off in the hills and many of my pupils lived miles away.

I taught that school for two years. It was in a poor district that people had named Hardscrabble. There was money enough for only six months of school each year. The other six months I worked. Meanwhile, Father had sold most of his stock, and, while he still operated our farm ranch, he had opened a retail store in Lexington. I spent the open time working in that store and studying law in the office of Captain Mc-Namar, a splendid and learned lawyer of the town. In fact, for eleven years I read law and haunted the courts in my spare time.

That portion of Nebraska was developing rapidly enough, but it was still thinly settled. All of the amusements we had we provided for ourselves. Wild fowl were everywhere, and nearly every man owned a gun and a hunting dog. We raced our horses, we broke wild ones and vied with each other in throwing a rope and shooting at a mark. Once each fall we had a coyote hunt. Scores of riders would circle a wide area and drive the poor yellow beasts towards a center where scores of them were slaughtered. Each young fellow aspired to possess a horse and buggy in which to drive his girl to picnics and to church.

People today would smile at our culture, but it was something vital and real to us. Nearly every neighborhood and town had a Lyceum or Literary Society. There we gathered on Friday nights to sing, speak pieces, act in dialogues and debate important questions. At first we argued affirmatively and negatively, "Resolved that there is more happiness in pursuit than in possession"; "Resolved that the saloon should be abolished." Once, after some of us had had a little college training, we very soberly debated the question "Resolved that the earth was flat," and proved that it was. I thought that father was the best debater in the community, but as he was quite dignified, spoke rather precise words and always wore black clothes and a white shirt in public, he usually was chosen to act as chairman or judge.

Those Literary Societies were the forerunner of the Chautauqua. Nearly every one did something. All of the people would sing, or try to, and the less tuneful voices waxed the loudest. I remember one huge cowboy who wore his hair long and had a mustache that must have measured fourteen inches from tip to tip. He would recite parodies on well-known rhymes in a singsong voice. For example, he took the "Old oaken bucket that hangs in the well," and made it read, "The dear little kittens, the sweet gentle kittens, the milk-loving kittens we drowned in the well." Another cowman, who wore four-inch heels and a flaxen mustache that almost equaled that of the first, would sing mournfully, "Oh bury me not on the lone prairie where wild coyotes would howl o'er me," and would play a prelude and interlude on a mouth organ.

Very few people were self-conscious as almost everyone was trying to sing, recite or play something. They made up original orations, recitations and songs. They played a fiddle, a mouth organ, a jew's-harp, a guitar or banjo, or a horn in the band. My father was a real good fiddler and played for dances. When he joined the Methodist Church, he eschewed "Old Zip Coon," "The Devil's Horn Pipe," and "The Irish Washerwoman," and often played sacred music instead.

When our economic troubles multiplied, we debated matters of great weight. Free Silver, Wall Street, the Populist Party and the Tariff engrossed our thoughts and forensic prowess. We would ride for many miles to attend a political meeting. Once when I was teaching, I rode my horse twenty-two miles in the evening to hear Bishop McCabe speak, and had to ride back in time for school the next morning. Our family traveled in a covered wagon for fifty miles to attend a G. A. R. reunion, where Senator Thurston was the chief attraction. Another time, about fifteen of us traveled in covered wagons sixty miles. We camped by our vehicles and cooked our meals at a fire of buffalo chips. It was a hard journey, through the hills, with only trails for roads. Going, returning and listening, we were a week on the way. We heard William Jennings Bryan and felt well rewarded for our efforts.

I would ride almost any distance to hear a congress-man or some other politician. I listened to so many of them with such avidity that I fear I almost memorized the words of their eloquence. The very man who sang "The Cowboy's Lament" with feeling was so much impressed by my eloquence that he staged a debate on Free Silver for me in a town more than twenty miles away. My opponent was a scholarly, dignified Colonel and I was a callow youth of seven-teen but I wore a Prince Albert coat. The two of us and the local band were the only attractions, but the hall was packed to the walls. I spoke with such im-passioned eloquence that people might have been swept off their feet had they not been standing so close together. Such was the enthusiasm that the school board met at once and elected me principal of the schools that boasted of a school bell and two teachers. Alas, how little the good men of the town knew the source of my burning words. The voice and ardor were mine, but I fear the arguments were largely those of the eloquent Judge Bill Green who was running for Congress, and to whom I had listened so often.

I was principal of that village school for two years. It seems to me that most of the young people of the time were forever seeking to find a way to express themselves in song and story, in home-talent plays and in oratory. Probably no one of us had heard an opera or a symphony orchestra or anything better than a traveling company playing "Uncle Tom's Cabin" or

"East Lynn." It is no wonder that we flocked to political meetings and regaled our talents in Literary Societies. There, in the warmth of our friends' applause, we were neither self-conscious nor afraid. Our boys tapped their boots in the rhythm of the local band. It sounded good for they had heard nothing better than the circus band.

When my two years were up I managed a period of study at the university, where I did nothing worthy of note but made both the debating and oratorical teams. I sketch some of the incidents that happened and the cultural impulses of the people I knew in my early years because they exerted a profound influence in the making of a nation that was just then really beginning to feel its own strength. All over rural America, where the larger share of the people of the nation lived, conditions were much the same. In an awakening power of the country, a yearning for knowledge and an impulse for creative effort, though scarcely recognized as such, were dominating the lives of the people.

It is quite different today. Now, entertainment is a major industry. Perhaps, in the aggregate of human hours absorbed, it may be the largest of all activities. But in each city, today, it is the same as in every other place. The people of the small town and the large city see the same moving pictures. They hear the same boogiewoogie or symphony on the radio. They listen, or pretend to listen, to the same high-minded radio speakers and to the same garrulous self-appointed prophets who attempt to analyze what they do not even understand themselves. There is much that is good and so much that is bad, and I suppose it was the same in the meetings and entertainments of other years. But there is a difference in then and now. People came out of the simple little Literary Societies happy and joyful and proud of their neighbors. They walked out of a Chautauqua tent with a new light in their eyes.

So it is interesting to study the reaction of an audience, or lack of it, to a modern moving picture. I marvel at the amazing spectacle of some screen productions. Again, I am puzzled with some of the dramatic offerings which, for popular purposes, are geared to a simple mind.

Often, most often, I think, people swarm from a wonderful theatre and such a performance sated and without expression on their faces. All of the commercialized entertainment, movies, radio and all the rest, could not have found a place in the imagination of the people fifty years ago. My greatest regret is that they have so dominated the abundant leisure of the people, and so filled the press with glamorous stories of performances, that there is but little incentive for people to do things for themselves.

In any event, when I returned from the university to Lexington, Nebraska, I went into business for myself. The country was growing fast. Land seekers came our way. I bought and sold lands and lots. I had a good office for abstracting and insurance that represented important landowners as well. I made money and could gratify my passion for good horses. I married and we led a most agreeable life. We went

to operas and symphonies, even traveled far to reach
them. I rarely missed a political convention and made
speeches at some of them. We all kept on with our
debates and home-talent shows.

In spite of my profit the cattle were murmuring
a bewitching song in my ear, and had a lure I could
not resist. All of my experience with the herds had
entailed much hardship and little profit. But I yearned
for the saddle as a drunkard longs for his cup. There
was no ease in my heart that was like the peace I
could find on the trail. I liked to ride afar. There
was no rest so sweet as that I could find sleeping
on a blanket laid on the ground, with my horse grazing
near, and one could fall asleep without first being
sleepy. One would awaken at night in the whispering
quiet of the resting herd while the stars were big and
near. The light would streak upwards through a
purple haze at dawn, like flaming daggers, and I could
watch the westward soaring of the morning star for
hours after the sun rose. In the sweep of the grazing
land there was space for thought and room for dreams.

I am not given to quote poetry but I often echoed
the lines of William Cullen Bryant:

These are the Gardens of the desert,
These, the unshorn fields, boundless and beautiful,
for which the speech of England has no name,
The Prairies.
I behold them for the first and my heart swells,
While the dilated sight takes in the encircling
    vastness.

Springtime on the prairie brought me a kind of peace I could not find, and never found, in any other place in the world. There was pure joy in the feeling that the winter storms had spent themselves without avail. Wild flowers, called forth, perhaps, by a thousand meadow larks, would come with the grass, and the viridity of the level land was grayed only by the horizon or skirting hills. It was the place not for sinful plow-shares, but for the cattle, and maybe the rider's dreams.

I acquired a couple of ranches of my own and operated others for clients. I got caught in the cattle depression of 1903 and I lost nearly all the money I had made. But business was good and in three or four years I recovered. In all of those years I was associated in a law office, and suddenly my wife and I decided that we would go to Lincoln, Nebraska, spend a year at the university, where Dean Pound told me he thought I could then pass the bar examinations.

Thus ended an era in my life, the like of which I, or no other man, will see again. Through the twenty years spent on the plains, my lean body had survived blizzards, sod houses and pneumonia. There had been labor and hungry days, with frozen clothes on my back and wet boots on my feet. But neither then, nor since, did they seem to be hard. The prairies, from the virgin sod, had been transformed into fertile and fruit-ful farms. Trees were growing along the open spaces and good roads had taken the place of the cattle paths. The worn ruts of the old Mormon trail, which took its straight course through the very pastures where my horse, Topsy, and I had galloped, had been plowed

under. Blistering hot winds and prairie fires had seared
nothing, but, perchance, our memory of them. It had
been a bounding, joy-filled and adventuresome twenty
years, when the men I knew thought they had to walk
on their own feet, if they walked at all, and make their
way for themselves. Who would not wish to live
through such days again?

All of those disconsolate and hopeless ones today,
who would have men to be nurtured by the Government,
and the pattern of their lives made a matter of public
care, should forgive some of the old-timers of a half
century ago, who knew no such thoughts, and would
have spurned such things.

Well, in any event, I was headed for the law, at
last, but I never reached the Promised Land.

THE CHAUTAUQUA MOVEMENT

There have been many books and stories written about the Chautauqua. I have read some of them. Some of the writers were quite sincere in their efforts to describe a vast movement. Others treated the matter with humor and occasionally with ridicule. Still others approached their subject with some condescension. No doubt they wrote what they felt or observed, or were told.

I have been asked by friends and publishers to write a history of the American Chautauquas. I have always been reluctant to attempt to do so. The task would involve much more research than I am capable of undertaking. Even then, much of the story would be undocumented to a great degree, for the larger share of the record of its scope and ideals rests only in the memory of its participants. Some eight years ago my own files, which completely filled an entire floor of a sizable building, were destroyed. In the current interest in the social and historic significance of the movement, that collection, if it were in existence, would have unusual value. It would have financial value for the collector as well, for in it were countless letters from presidents and princes, from philosophers and poets, from college presidents and maybe charlatans. There were letters from senators and scientists. Governors, congressmen, Chambers of Commerce, community welfare workers, clergymen, soldiers, artists, actors, and, most zestful and heartening of all, thousands of eager, ardent and hopeful letters from boys and girls.

The Chautauqua movement, in its enlarged form, began with the establishment of the circuit Chautauquas. A circuit comprised, say, sixty to a hundred towns. The program in each town began one day later than its predecessor, from first to last. The first two of the approximately one hundred circuits began operations in 1907. Mr. Keith Vawter was the manager of one, the larger of the two, and I was the manager of the other. Vawter has been dead for a number of years. At this point it is quite fitting to mention another man who made an indelible impression upon the ideals of the movement and must surely be reckoned as a pioneer in it. That man is Mr. J. Roy Ellison, who later became co-owner and manager of a large system. In the beginning Ellison was manager of the booking department of Independent Chautauqua programs for the Redpath Lyceum Bureau. He and Vawter made some experiments in the preliminary organizing of a circuit. The chief motive of these experiments was to dispose of surplus dates of attractions for which they had contracts.

A discussion of those early efforts usually results in arguments concerning the date of the first circuit. The matter is not very important but in the years preceding the actual beginning of a well-organized circuit, Vawter and Ellison were clearly pioneers. They were not alone, although their work in 1904 to 1906 was perhaps the most important. However, other high-minded gentlemen were making important explorations in what came to be a very great field. Many of them, along with Vawter and Ellison, deserve much more attention than I am able to give to them. Anyhow these early efforts were recorded thoughtfully and quite thoroughly in a work by Mr. Hugh Orchard, published in 1923, and entitled *Fifty Years of Chautauqua*.

No later managers ever conceived and held to higher ideals than the ones expressed by those pioneers. However, in operations and policies I can find but little similarity in theirs and of those who came later.

When I think of the large number of men who became Chautauqua managers, I falter in the task before me. I think I knew them all, most of them quite intimately. They who are alive, and the memory of those who no longer live, have a large place in my affections. Those men were great and good people. They met together often and discussed their policies, sometimes their finances, but always they spoke mostly of their ideals. I affirm that their chief interest was to serve the people they entertained. I falter in my task because I cannot ascribe to them individually the high praise that is their due.

They were good clean citizens and master salesmen, but with all their ability they could not have operated so vast a project if the way had not been provided by uncounted thousands of local efforts for self-improvement and public enlightenment.

I have been informed by the president and the director of libraries of the Iowa State University that their fine institution is making a collection of Chautauqua papers, and I know no one better fitted to the task, for Iowa was of the very center of the far-flung range of the Chautauqua tents. What I write now shall be drawn from my own experience and knowledge and observation. In due time, no doubt, under the ministrations of the University at Iowa City, a true and comprehensive history will be written. As for me, while I am reckoned as a pioneer in the dramatic growth of the Chautauqua, my viewpoint is like that of the multitudes who thronged the hot big tops, for I am of the same people as the millions who sat on the hard benches in the too often blistering summer heat.

My background was cast in happy, hopeful struggle, in hardship and bad weather. I would be a poor specimen of an American if I had not had in my soul some instinct of the pioneer, since three generations of us had spanned a portion of three centuries and most of the years that made the sum were lived on the frontiers. Before I began Chautauqua work, the forces that moved me along had been shouting that a man should walk on his own feet, that he should pay his debts; that the Government and the Constitution were high and noble, and worthy of his complete loyalty and obedience. That the Church and School were dominant factors in life, and that the Community was his America, in form and substance, and it was his duty to find an honorable part in it. That is a fair statement of ideals as they were revealed to me and, I think, they were quite commonly shared by the people I know so well throughout the Midwest.

To engage in politics was regarded as an inherited right and it was one freely exercised by the men of my day. They would shout "turn the rascals out" loud enough during political campaigns, but a thought, if it ever came to any one, that the form of government should be changed, or even modified, or be colored by any custom or belief not rooted in "the great American people," was as abhorrent as the devil himself. There can, in truth, be found much to criticize in the community pride in those Midwestern towns and cities. It was a pride not free from vanity, of course, nor from some intolerance. Nevertheless it was a pride in which both local and personal ambition were surely joined.

There was a constant desire for more and better schools. Education was ardently longed for and some form of self-expression a freed instinct. These accounted for all of the literary societies, and the fine reception given to lecturers from afar. I do not think I detract from the worth of the cultural aspirations in that era when I admit that they were too often vague in concept. How frequently, fifty years ago, and since, these words were spoken with a firm jaw, albeit from the depths of frustration and mental starvation: "I want to work hard and give my children a good education so they will not need to work as hard as I do." However sincere were the legions of ambitious parents who uttered the words, they were sowing sad seeds from which have been reaped much unhappiness and discontent. Could they but have known that the attainment of knowledge is its own justification and need not necessarily be reflected in ease and better bank accounts, and that fruitful honest labor is the source of man's greatest happiness! They come, as men always will come, to realize that as they moved into the lengthening shadows of their lives, they cherish best of all the pleasant memories of the days when they toiled hardest.

We had a Lyceum course in Lexington, Nebraska, each winter of the last few years that I lived there. Because of the nature of my activities and my ardent interest in it I was a member, and, part of the time, manager of the sponsoring committee. This committee was composed of the men who assumed the financial responsibility, did the advertising, sold the tickets, and if they did not sell enough they would need to make up the deficit from their own pockets, although I cannot remember that we ever had a loss. We would sign a contract with the Redpath Lyceum Bureau for the appearance of the attractions we selected. It was called the Lyceum, but everyone spoke of it as a lecture course. We would have at intervals through the winter, perhaps three lecturers, a musical company and an entertainer, maybe a cartoonist or chalk talker, or a humorist. They were very popular and interesting, and I have no doubt most people would enjoy them even in these sophisticated days.

No narrative of the Lyceum and Chautauqua could be written without reference to the Redpath Lyceum Bureau. It was the first one to be established and it was founded in Boston in 1868, by James Redpath.

Redpath was born on the Scottish side of Berwick-on-tweed in 1833, and emigrated with his family to America in 1850. He became a printer and then a newspaperman and joined the staff of Horace Greeley on the *Tribune* when he was nineteen. He served intermittently on that paper for nearly thirty years. Redpath was an ardent abolitionist and a crusader of all sorts. He went to Kansas, got acquainted with John Brown and wrote a life of the Osawatomie leader within thirty days after the latter was hanged for treason at Harpers Ferry. He published a paper in Kansas, reported the Civil War for various newspapers, and after the Confederate surrender, was for a time superintendent of schools in Charleston, South Carolina.

It was at this place that he initiated the custom of decorating the graves of Union soldiers, which later became Decoration Day. Redpath wrote a number of books and assisted Mark Twain in writing his autobiography, and the former Confederate President, Jefferson Davis, in preparing his memoirs.

The Lyceum, in the sense of employing outside or professional speakers, was, of course, the outgrowth of the literary societies of New England. Such societies were altogether local affairs, without any thought or plan of confederation with other communities. Many men and women of fame and fine repute were traveling about to deliver their lectures for pay, but there was no type of organized management, and fees were variable and often very low. Indeed, it is said that the great Ralph Waldo Emerson, at first, would make an address for as little as five dollars and three quarts of oats for his horse. Emerson, Wendell Phillips, Horace Greeley, Charles Sumner and many other notable speakers were looking to the platform for a hearing, but it was the tour of Charles Dickens, the English novelist, that gave Redpath his incentive to organize his Bureau. Dickens had found that lecture arrangements were most difficult to make, and he and his friend Dolby had a "Dickens" of a job completing the plans. So Redpath founded the Boston Bureau, and later the name was changed to the Redpath Bureau.

The founder enjoyed great success because he had the confidence of the eminent platform people of those expansive days, and his organization was very convenient for the lecture committees which were springing up all over the country. He sold his interests in 1875 to George Hathaway and Major J. B. Pond, and the Bureau continued through days that were both better and worse under various kinds of management until 1902, when it was acquired by Crawford Peffer, Keith Vawter and George Hathaway. By that time, however, many other Bureaus had come into existence and competition was very keen. Some Bureaus had but a brief existence, but a number of others managed by brilliant men grew to be powerful and useful. Perhaps few, if any, and not even Redpath, were based on a very sound economic policy, but they paid their debts, and practically all, if they finally closed their books, left no list of disappointed creditors.

The Chautauqua was no doubt the fruit of the Lyceum, but it was more expansive in idea, and surely more nearly religious and educational in concept. It was named, of course, for Lake Chautauqua, a peaceful, beautiful body of water in the State of New York. The first Chautauqua, or what would really be called *the* Chautauqua, was founded on the shore of the lake in 1874 by the enlightened Bishop John H. Vincent, and Lewis Miller of the Methodist Church. It was, and is named, Chautauqua Institution, for it has maintained its fine service and healthful sessions for eighty years. Visitors went there from all parts of the United States, to enjoy the speakers, the music, the reading courses and religious services, as well as a pleasant vacation in camp. Some of them brought back glowing praise of the fine assembly, to their own communities. Here and there an ambitious local group, inspired by the good Bishop's example, a pretty lake or a grove of trees, and their own surging desire for culture and enlightenment, would organize their members to provide a summer assembly or Chautauqua of their own. They expected to draw heavily from a wide area, and were not disappointed. On their "big" days, notably on Sundays, the railroads would sometimes run special trains on which the visitors could ride for a low fare, and on almost any day there were hardly enough livery stables and hitching posts to accommodate the horses of the out-of-town guests.

A part of the Chautauqua grounds was turned into a camp, which they called their "tent city." Small tents were rented for those who wished to live in the camp. These were twelve by fourteen or fourteen by sixteen feet in size, and for a dollar or so extra a wooden floor would be installed. Many of the campers would cook their meals on oil stoves, and for others there was a public "dining hall," often in a big tent.

There wasn't much in the way of sports and games, except where there was a lake, and in such cases boats were to be had. To use the expression nearly everyone used at the time, "It was a feast of reason and flow of soul." The meetings were held in a large wooden auditorium, or if none had been erected, a huge tent was rented from a tent and awning company. But wood or canvas, the place was spoken of as The Tabernacle, after the style of the many religious Camp Meetings which everyone knew about. Classes for reading courses, Bible, cooking, and current events were held in the forenoons and late afternoons. The big events were the afternoon and evening programs which were designed to be popular, but always inspirational.

For each program there was a concert which was called a prelude, and then a lecture by some man widely advertised, although if the concert company was particularly large and expensive, sometimes it would give a whole program. Practically all of these companies and lecturers were booked from Bureaus, and were paid fees for their services. For the sake of economy these paid attractions were retained for two or more days, and some of them were put to it to provide sufficient repertoire for the whole engagement and there were many "by request" numbers sung or played. The concert companies were of various types. There would be, perhaps, Jubilee Singers, with seven or eight colored men and women, an instrumental ensemble nearly al-

ways classed as an orchestra, occasionally the local
band, or a mixed aggregation of men and women,
singing, playing instruments and doing all sorts of
things, and inevitably a male quartette. In fact some
of the critics in later days, when the Chautauqua had
spread itself all over the country, complained that the
male quartette was the only thing indigenous to the
Chautauqua. They were mistaken, as I may be able
to show before I am through. In any event, some of
the male quartettes became so well known that they
achieved a fine reputation that was almost national.
The Kentucky Colonels, the Wesleyan Quartette, the
Dunbar Singers and Bell Ringers, the Hesperians,
and the Chicago Quartette were some of them.

Besides the musicians and the lecturers each Chautauqua made it a point to provide one or more single
attractions classed as entertainers. Entertainer was
a word that might be hard to understand today as it
was thought of forty years ago. He might be a magi-
cian like the Great Laurant, or Germaine who sometimes covered the vaudeville circuit and made the Big
Time. Such a man would have quite a company of
assistants in uniform, and a wealth of settings and
properties that filled the stage. Or he may have been
a humorist like Ralph Bingham or Jess Pugh, or a
reader of plays like Adrian Newens, Leland Powers,
Elias Day who did about everything with the spoken
word, Isabelle Garhill Beecher, or Katharine Ridgway.
The art of the people in this class reached a high point.
Many people on the benches listened to a play quite
well portrayed by a single actor, who somehow managed

to make the drama very real and moving. Other entertainers were like Sidney Landon, and were called make-up artists. They would apply grease paint and wigs and don costumes of a sort, while speaking their lines, and in the end would appear as Mark Twain or Longfellow or Tennyson. It was all exceedingly clever, and their work brought forth many gasps from the audience. I doubt if there really are any such artists today who have reached so far towards perfection. I do not think their kind will be seen again because electric lights, amplifiers, sound effects and stage settings now furnish a large share of a compelling illusion which those of other days had to provide with their own forms and faces and personalities.

But the basic idea of the Chautauqua was to give the speaker his hour. The men who pioneered the great adventures in glimpses into the outside world, saw to that. No whistling nor clapping of hands nor sighs at the reluctant but final bows of the entertainers and male quartette could serve to delay the lecturer, or to lessen his importance. He provided the force that made sponsors labor without stint, neglect their own affairs and face the peril of paying deficits. So long as he could furnish the supreme motive for effort the Chautauqua grew to astounding size, and when, a quarter of a century later, he was shunted about in the impact of shows and lighter entertainment, the Chautauqua waned and finally disappeared. There were, to be sure, other causes for languor in the tents, some of which I will finally try to reveal.

The entrepreneur of the Chautauqua was wont to proclaim that he was furnishing all varieties of lecturers. That was scarcely true, although in subject and in chosen fields his list was variable enough. There were clergymen, simple reverends and bishops; scientists, explorers; college presidents and professors; judges, lawyers and politicians; writers and women. There is a variety of a kind in any group of men, but there was one pattern every Chautauqua lecturer had to fit if he secured many return dates, no matter how much fame or success he had achieved in his own vocation. He might be erudite, or without a university degree. He might be a wise and famous judge from the bench, a traveler who spoke many tongues, a senator or governor, a candidate for the presidency of the United States, or the author of many books, but with all he had to be inspirational, and most of them were, in varying degrees. I flinch, even yet, as I write that word. It was a hackneyed word, glibly spoken, and paraphrased as "Mother, home and heaven." I have puzzled myself to define it according to the concept expressed, or merely felt, by the Chautauqua audience. As nearly as I can interpret it, it was the quality in the speaker's life and demeanour and words that made men and women want to freshen their ambitions, to aspire a little higher, to become better neighbors and friends, to clean up the town a bit, to kiss the children when they returned to their homes, and perhaps to pray a little more. That is the definition I constructed from the words spoken to me by thousands of people, first and last, and from the shining eyes of the crowds that swarmed from the Chautauqua tent. Emotionalism? I won't deny it. What great leader can you find in all time who would not make an emotional appeal?

The local Chautauquas were growing in number, particularly during the first half-dozen years of this century. The estimates that have been made of their numbers were inaccurate. It was thought that there were many hundreds, although it would have been a simple matter to make a correct count. I had occasion to know of most of them, if in no other way than from the correspondence of William Jennings Bryan, to whose letters I eventually had access. I have kept no records, but I believe there were about one hundred and fifty well-established assemblies in the country in 1906. These were distributed well, chiefly in the Middle West from Ohio to Nebraska, and from Minnesota to Kentucky, although there were some without those rough limits. The duration of a Chautauqua ranged from ten days, which was almost the rule, to several weeks as in the case of the Mother Chautauqua.

The most important Chautauqua in Nebraska was the Epworth Assembly in Lincoln, which some of us in Lexington would attend. We were so much impressed by the Lincoln programs, the large attendance there, and by the success of our own lecture course, that we organized for ourselves. We had our first session in 1904, under a share expenses plan with the Redpath Lyceum Bureau, which, apparently, had overbought in its list of talent. Although I was a member of the

committee, I did not give much time to it that year,
because that was the summer of my marriage. During
the next two years, however, I was secretary and gave
a great deal of attention to the enterprise. We had no
lake, nor even a good-sized pond. But we had a city
park, a well-wooded area, to which no one had given
much attention, and it was fenced but well undergrown.
When we cleared away the undergrowth and installed
water hydrants here and there, most people were surprised to find what a pleasant place it was. We had a
splendid attendance in 1905 and 1906 and quit each
session with money in the bank. I was impressed by
the worth of our "talent," but felt very sorry for some
of them, their travel had been so hard. One of our
headliners, 1906, was Captain Richmond Pearson Hobson, the hero of the *Merrimac* in the Cuban Bay. We
were near enough to the Spanish American War to have
great admiration for the brave naval officer. Hobson
captivated our people completely. He was a handsome
and graceful figure and a facile speaker. He quite won
Lexington's heart, when after a few sentences that
hot afternoon, he paused and then said, "By the way,
do you mind if I take off my coat? I can make a
speech if I wear it, but I think I will make a better one
if I remove it." There were plenty of coatless men in
the audience, but I am quite sure no one was so im-
maculate in his limited attire as our speaker. I had
a visit with Hobson afterwards, and was anxious to
learn all he could tell me about the Chautauquas. His
traveling experience was similar to others. His last

engagement had been in Wisconsin, and from Lexington he was to proceed to Kentucky for the next.

It was then and there I acquired a very keen desire to help in some way to avoid so much waste in time and travel. From what I knew and believed of other communities, there was a good market for the offerings of the platform. My plans to move to Lincoln were made. I was nearly finished in the job of selling my business and property, and I had rented a house in Lincoln. While in this state, I wrote to the Redpath Lyceum Bureau, at Chicago, and expressed some of my thoughts regarding the desirability of organizing to eliminate some of the waste. I received a reply at once from Keith Vawter, asking me to meet him in Omaha to talk the matter over. I went to a conference which resulted in a complete change of my plans, and an entirely new direction in my life. I was quite enthused with the idea of organizing a number of Chautauquas within a fairly limited territory, making use of the same attractions for all, and under single direction. I found that Vawter was far ahead of me in thought and, indeed, in his plans. He had, as I related, in effect, already made an experiment or two, motivated in part by the necessity of disposing of unsold dates of talent he held under guaranteed contract. He was preparing to move his headquarters from Chicago to Cedar Rapids, Iowa, and establish a circuit with the latter city as a center. He was quite well along in his arrangements and had engaged some men for the promotion work. Of course I favored the idea, but

I felt that the guarantee he wanted from the individual city was too heavy in the number of season tickets that had to be sold. He expected to prevail upon local citizens to agree to sell or pay for one thousand tickets at a dollar and fifty cents, and he would furnish a program for six days, the necessary equipment and all the advertising, in short a ready-made Chautauqua. His proposed program was rather light, I thought, but he said he would be prepared to add to it if occasion required. I objected to so short a session because I believed that no community would want to do without a Sunday, always a big day, and a thousand season tickets were too many. I favored a smaller number at a higher price. He had given much thought to the matter and was quite determined to proceed according to plan. Nevertheless, as I was so enthusiastic about the idea, he appeared to be quite anxious to have me associated with him although my whole experience had been found in Lexington; apparently he thought I had some money to back up my own ideas, although that factor never made much difference with him. In the end, he offered me a fair salary with some options for commissions, and had been so sure of himself and of my interest that he had a contract already prepared. I finally signed the paper. Out of my life flew all my plans for the law, and, anyhow, the great Dean Pound had responded to a call for wider fields. I had no regrets, nor have I yet. All the time I had spent reading law was well invested, I am sure, and what I had learned has enriched my life.

I worked less than two months under that contract, and did not draw a dollar of the salary provided for, although Vawter once offered to pay in full. After I had established my wife and baby in Lincoln, I traveled industriously, booking Redpath attractions at the local Chautauquas, which, after the advent of the circuits, came to be called independent or old-line assemblies. Although the booking season was well spent, I was quite successful in that field, and besides secured a number of Lyceum contracts, so that on the whole my commissions amounted to as much as I would have made in salary. The simple fact is that I wanted to establish a circuit of my own, and Vawter was extremely sympathetic and co-operative. I was courting some good cities as I went about, and finally secured local Chautauqua organizations in ten of them. At first we planned to add these to Vawter's circuit, which was progressing pretty well, but as our plans were different and I had promised each a session of nine days, we decided to make my places into a circuit, although a short one. Vawter was helpful all the time. He had access to platform people, which would have required a long time for me to obtain.

I think it would be wise to digress for a moment to take a little turn in nomenclature. From that Omaha meeting Keith Vawter and I were sending forth the first ripples of a tide that swept the whole nation, extended well into Canada and spread to far-off Australia and New Zealand. Names and titles came without bid and fixed themselves upon the groups that became the components of the Chautauqua.

Those who performed—lecturer, musician, entertainer or actor—were the Talent. No other title was ever found for them, no matter how hard some tried to find a more graceful and definitive name. The owners were the Managers, which was near enough to the truth. The hard-muscled lads who did the physical work of erecting the tents, building the seats and stage, man the box office and take the tickets at the entrance, were the Crew, and a chapter should be written concerning them. The bright-eyed young women, teachers for the most part, to whose care was entrusted the vexing management of flocks of juveniles, were the Junior Girls. Those who pushed forward into countless towns, to sell the idea, and get signatures on the dotted line, long before the coming of the Talent, were the Agents. The local citizens, who from motives of city pride, community betterment, or even under the persuasion of a good salesman, signed the contracts, well knowing they were hazarding both hard work and their dollars, were the Committees. There was another class. It was composed of bright energetic men, young men mostly, and they were the Platform Managers. Some of us tried to call them Superintendents. One circuit named them Directors, but the days of the local Chautauqua had fastened the name of Platform Managers upon them, and that title stuck to the end.

The men who followed in the wake of the Agent, who helped to organize the Committees, and sell the tickets and distribute the advertising, were of course the Advance Men.

Leaving people for a moment, the adjunctive tents in which the Crew lived, stored the properties and sometimes prepared them as dressing rooms for the Talent, were the Pup Tents. Later, as progress was made, the stage end of the big tent was made large enough to provide sleeping and dressing room space under the Big Top. Even though the Chautauqua became ambitious enough to present plays that had the mark of "Broadway success," and operas and musical comedies, our rostrum was never a stage but the Platform.

Of all the groups, four of them were the ones that were always in attendance at round tables, conventions and the annual meetings of the International Lyceum and Chautauqua Association. The four were Talent, Managers, Committees and Agents.

My circuit, that first year, the summer of 1907, opened at Blair, Nebraska, and all of its members were confined to Nebraska. Mr. Vawter's first, the same summer, extended pretty well through Iowa and Missouri. He remained steadfast to his plan of six-day sessions with his basic talent alike throughout, although he augmented his lists considerably with added headliners. My programs were drawn more from the open dates of time blocks of talent, part of whose time I had sold here and there. In the very beginning we both inaugurated a policy, which when successfully effected, proved to be the sustaining factor which, to a great degree, insured the continuance of the Chautauqua for more than twenty years. Without it the movement would have had a shorter, and certainly a more hazardous, existence. The most difficult and expensive process in perfecting arrangements for a large chain of towns was the securing of the contract, which involved much labor and uncertainty. So at the first we trained our platform managers to renew the agreement during the current session.

Our first year's efforts were rewarded with some success in this respect, and with huge acclaim so far as popular approval was concerned. We both were the losers in money. Mr. Vawter had had to curtail his ancient booking operations because of the time his circuit required. A brilliant young man, Harry P. Harrison, from Iowa, was sold an interest in the Redpath Bureau, had taken charge of the office in Chicago, and was showing great managerial promise. As for me, I had to draw upon my commissions for living and used some of my cash reserve in the initial operation of the circuit. But I think we both felt confident, and believed that our experiments proved, that with a finer organization we could achieve a financial as well as a popular success.

There was one thing that both Vawter and I were sure about: we were going ahead. We had not found the answer to our financial problems, and clearly had not demonstrated that the Chautauqua circuit could pay out, let alone yield a profit. But we knew what had to be accomplished before we could avoid loss and perhaps make something for ourselves. Losses in our first year, 1907, and again in 1908, could be traced

to definite causes. In order to secure enough towns
to fill out a determined season we were forced to accept
a few faulty contracts, where local responsibility had
not been fully assumed, and likewise some partial
guarantees. That would not do for long, whether we
had profit or loss. It was a matter of ethics to treat
all cities alike, and we knew that confidence could not
be retained indefinitely with a majority of communities
yielding its full quota in advance season-ticket sales,
while a few were allowed to participate for a lesser
amount.

We needed to be more closely in touch with our
towns, not only for a week or two, but, to a degree,
during the whole year. We had to perfect local organizations, and we must find a way to reduce expenses without loss of quality in our program. Besides
there were eight or nine months, from September until
June, during which we must invest in the salaries
and expenses of agents and all the other things for
which we knew cash would be needed before we could
reap any harvest. Vawter had a good going business
in his Lyceum and independent Chautauqua bookings,
but he was sure the proceeds would not be enough to
finance him through the long period before he would
again put his tents into the field. I was even worse
provided for, although I still had some cash I had
earned in Lexington.

I was anxious to apply the circuit idea to the Lyceum
and arranged for the exclusive use of that part of
Nebraska that lies north of the Platte River. Generally I offered a course at a fixed price, which was

extremely low, expecting to book my attractions so closely that travel and selling costs could be reduced by two-thirds. The venture was successful. I had more lecture courses in that area, by five times over, than had ever before been booked in any year within the whole state. It was another proof of the economic promise in the circuit plan.

Mr. Vawter formed a corporation, separate from the Redpath Bureau, for the operation of his circuit. It was named the Redpath, and later the Redpath-Vawter Chautauqua System. We incorporated my share of the business under the name of the Western Redpath Chautauqua System. I engaged a few good agents and through the winter and spring of 1907-08 managed to secure nearly seventy city members for my circuit in Nebraska and Kansas. Vawter clung to the idea of a six-day session, although he had complaints from some places that had no Sunday program. A basic factor in our plan was to schedule our talent throughout the season with no open dates. We contracted with the talent on the basis of an agreed salary per week, and knew we would have to pay them in full whether they performed or not. In his plan he needed three units of talent, that is three musical companies, and three groups each of entertainers and lecturers, and each attraction was scheduled for two days in each city. Interspersed with these he added his headliners, and since each of these was booked for a single lecture, he and I could share their time.

As for me, I compromised with eight-day sessions, and therefore had four units and the added famous people. I can give no better idea of one of my programs that year than to write an outline of the talent that appeared on our platform in Fort Scott, Kansas, in the eight-day session beginning on July 7, 1908, omitting all the printed glowing words of praise with which they were heralded in advance.

The Hesperian Male Quartette, four men who had formed themselves into a singing group in Chicago University twelve years before. Two of their members were professional lecturers, and three were or had been preachers.

The Kirksmiths, four charming girls, three of whom were sisters. This bright group had graced my platforms two or three years, and as other sisters in the family became old enough they were added one at a time until there were six. These young people went into vaudeville and enjoyed rich success for a long time.

The Sterling Jubilee Singers with four men and three women, all colored, of course, and singing the old camp meeting and Jubilee songs which I think I would like to hear again.

The Royal Hungarian Orchestra. It is strange how many "Royals" and "Imperials," a democratic people like to attach to the names of their entertainers and merchandise. There were eight men in the group and undoubtedly they made pleasing melody.

In entertainers, there were two, one at least, of whom became famous and his name almost a household word all over the country. He is Adrian Newens, and even then he was a veteran. Currently he was the head of the Department of Speech in Iowa State College, a

fine Agricultural Institution at Ames. He was present-
ing two plays, "A Singular Life" and "A Message
from Mars," from which he achieved just fame, and I
think he graced the platform for nearly a half of a
century, and is good yet.

The other was Gilbert Eldredge, an impersonator
and make-up performer who called forth much hilarity
and the kind of laughs any man likes to hear and
join in.

Interpolated for three evenings, we had moving pictures. That doesn't sound important today, but was
fairly sensational in 1908. The pictures were presented by an operator from the American Vitagraph
Company. Probably but a small percentage of the
audience had ever before seen a motion picture. The
films were as droll and old fashioned as you can imagine, and specialized in huge crowds chasing themselves
or something else down the street, falling and tumbling
around, and their antics evoked such screams of merri-
ment the customers could scarcely sit on their benches.
The people needed some of such ridiculous comedy if
they were to digest all the lectures provided.

Twelve lecturers were on the program, and some of
them gave two lectures each. I must name them, if
for no other reason than to indicate the capacity of the
people to absorb eloquence.

J. Mohammed Ali, born a Mohammedan in Punjab,
India, educated at a university in the Far East, con-
verted to Christianity, who revealed many facts concerning his land and people.

William Rainey Bennet, who, like Newens, became a star platform attraction, and was constantly in high demand as long as the Chautauquas lived.

Hugh A. Orchard, a Christian minister, a poet and writer of some note, and quite a philosopher.

Judge Lee S. Estelle, from the district bench of Omaha, a former high official in the National G. A. R., and a deep student of crime and juvenile delinquency. Poor little devils, we were working on them even then.

George McNutt, known far and wide as "The Full Dinner Pail" man, a quaint and earnest philosopher, who knew all the trials and triumphs of unskilled laborers, and was wholesome for any one. With McNutt was a bright little boy, his son, Pat, who never got enough of visiting with the crew, and swinging on the tent ropes. Pat became a well-known and successful author and playwright, as many of you know.

Doctor Monroe Markley, a gifted and handsome Congregational minister, and an adept in heart to heart talks.

Carl D. Thompson, who had a strong leaning towards Socialism, which very few knew anything about in that period, although he did not talk about that. He, too, was a preacher.

Colonel Robert S. Seeds, a farmer's man, who had made much scientific study of soils, and was rated as a humorous lecturer.

Dr. Peter MacQueen, explorer and world traveler, who had been with Stanley in Darkest Africa, was a Fellow in various scientific societies, an old friend of Theodore Roosevelt. It was said that he and Richard

Harding Davis were the only honorary members of "The
Rough Riders." His lecture was illustrated by many
stereopticon pictures, a kind of diversion very popular
in those days. However, MacQueen was in Africa
when we engaged him, suffered from fever, and a finger bitten by a wild beast, and if my recollection is accurate, he did not return in time for his tour, and a substitute had to be found. Meanwhile the stories of his
adventures grew and grew until some people were led
to believe a whole arm had been devoured, but when
he finally appeared a year later only a part of one finger
was missing.

The substitution was a fortunate one. I was able
to secure Henry George, Jr., son of the Great Single
Tax exponent. He was used to being a substitute, because he had been nominated to be mayor of New York,
to take the place of his great father on the ticket, when
the latter died in the midst of the campaign. The
younger George was elected to Congress, and was more
or less a radical in his economic views, but I have no
doubt that the same opinions would be deemed quite
conservative today. Henry was one of the most likable
and charming men I have ever known. He was most
meticulous in all things. He would not appear without evening dress, and he observed all the social niceties. He told me that since he held economic ideas contrary to those of most other people, he was particular to
conform to all recognized social customs.

Then came the lecturers whose names were printed
in big type, and there were three of them. They were,
I should say, the headliners.

George L. Sheldon, the Republican Governor of Nebraska. He was a sturdy individual, and had been educated in Nebraska University and in Harvard. He was tall and fine-looking, and was making a good executive for his state.

Judge Ben B. Lindsey of the Juvenile Court of Denver, already famous, with a great heart and boundless sympathy for mankind. I have sat in his court, and in chambers, where he really heard most of his cases, and I have never had a finer or more wholesome and spiritually healthful experience elsewhere.

The last one of the stars was the Honorable Warren G. Harding, Lieutenant Governor of Ohio. I think I must presently say more of him, but from the beginning we expected him to make quite a name for himself and it is significant that in the announcements we made, after recounting some of the honors he had gained, it was stated that "other honors await his beck and call."

Besides the above, the booklet of the Chautauqua promised a course of educational lectures, one daily, by Professor D. M. Bowen.

That was the mental, concordant, and risible bill of fare we offered to the people of Fort Scott, and anyone of them could have it all, if he bought a season ticket for $2.00, and he could buy one for a child for a dollar. He who came only occasionally need pay twenty-five to fifty cents for each visit.

With such an aggregation, we moved through the summer and ended in McCook, Nebraska, August thirtieth. I remember the date, because on that day the tent blew down and I received word of the birth of my second daughter, Eleanor.

We got our tents and properties headed for storage, dismissed the weary crews, and after I had visited my little family for a day or so, I met Keith Vawter at St. Joseph, but not until I had had a balance sheet of the season's operations. The first question I asked him was "How did you come out?" He said he had lost something between seventy-five hundred and ten thousand dollars, and I said that made me feel better for that represented about what I believed our own deficit to be. The grim fact was that I was getting painfully low in cash, and much pondering of future plans was indicated. In the meantime I had arranged to buy Vawter's interest in the Western Redpath System, which was re-incorporated as Redpath-Horner Chautauquas, and had the purchase sum as an additional obligation, which, somehow, I contrived to pay not too long afterwards.

We were to be partners no longer in business operations, but we were joined in spirit and counsel and deep friendship for many years.

Keith Vawter was an odd man in the sense that he would never try to be, nor think, nor act like any one else. His temperament was usefully complementary to mine. He was coldly reasoning, masterful in planning, and when he had made a plan nothing could cause him to deviate from it. He wore none of his virtues on his sleeve and, if for no other reason than stubbornness, he submerged the evidence of his finest traits. He was unaffected and realistic. In his choice of friends he could not brook mental snobbery nor habits of exaggeration, but frankly made use of men who possessed such traits if they had other values useful for his purpose. His words of praise were scant for any one, and some thought they were complimented if they escaped his sarcasm. There was poor hunting for talent seeking commendation from him.

There was one lecturer whose highest ambition seemed to be achieved when he was engaged for one of Vawter's circuits. The chap was sincere enough but he had a high self-esteem and made but little effort to conceal his own good opinion of himself. He was given to indulge in poetic flights of eloquence even if at the cost of facts.

Next to the attainment of his opportunity to lecture for the great Vawter, the man desired most the presence of the astute manager in his audience and made all efforts to secure it. He wrote many letters and transmitted verbal messages to Vawter saying how much honored he would be if his manager would come to hear him speak. The long trail was well shortened before Vawter appeared. Characteristically, but patiently enough, Keith sat in the shade of a tree outside the tent and whittled a stick without once looking at the speaker. When the rhetorical tide had subsided and there was no response from his chief, the speaker, unable to compose his eagerness, found Vawter and used all his wiles to draw out a voluntary expression. When none was offered, he finally asked point blank, "Well, Mr. Vawter, how did you like my lecture?" Vawter looked him over and finally said, "Your lecture? It reminded me of a Ford car." That was in the days of the revolutionary Model T, more noted for its efficiency than for physical ease for the passenger. The poor lad sought to find solace in the opinion although he would have been happier if he had let well enough alone. "A Ford car," he puzzled. "Why is it like that?" "It made me tired in the same place," said Vawter. The man with his sarcasm could puncture fancies and deflate self-blown affectation more effectively than any one else I have ever known.

He would establish no rules of conduct for his men. He said they knew what the Chautauqua stood for and that it tried to conform to all the recognized conventions of his great family of communities, and if any man of his got himself clouded with a breath of scandal, he, Vawter, might feel badly if the man were guiltless, but off the payroll he went. All through his career he was sternly and consistently honest. A few of us who saw him often and knew him best, were conscious of fine attributes hidden from many. He gave from his inherent kindness and from his money freely, and as silently, as he was quiet in all his ways.

Vawter was the son of a well-known Christian minister. He was a graduate of Drake University, and sometime chairman of the board of his Alma Mater. He had strange political acumen, a fine talent for organization, and possessed self-created ideals which he never, or rarely, expressed in words. When he retired from his Chautauqua work, he amused himself on his Iowa farm and in his village bank, until the end of his life. He is very poorly credited as the man who initiated the circuit plan for the Chautauqua.

As for me I was fortunate at last to find the formula for operation and design which, I think, was adopted and used by all of the numerous systems for twenty years, or until the big tents were struck for the last time.

SYSTEMATIZING THE SYSTEM

The general plan for the operation of my circuit was good, but the experience of the first two years indicated faults which must be corrected. I knew well enough that our programs must not be reduced in quality but must become more pleasing, rather than less, if we held the interest of the committees, upon the co-operation of whom our life depended. Besides the merit of the individual attractions, the co-ordination of the various units with each other must be improved. No one at the table likes to eat soup or salad with his ice cream. I wanted to find a plan by which the units might be mutually complementary and each have the place, in the order of appearance, best suited to its worth.

Unless we could be satisfied to serve merely as a purveyor of entertainment and good cheer, we had to establish some symphonic order based upon a flexible but good intellectual idea. The movements of the parts in the program did not allow such arrangements. All the cities of the circuit had to be divided into a series of groups, each group comprising four places, and each of the four had to be within easy travel distance to each of the other three. This gave little or no latitude in assigned dates. If a certain city found a particular week undesirable because of local conditions, nevertheless it was almost necessary to accept that week. As for us, we could not take advantage of a main line of a railroad where train service was excellent, but moving in a restricted circle we must depend upon branches where sometime there were only one or two trains a day. But, most grievous, we had a disorderly schedule of appearance. One attraction might be best suited to open a session, but not nearly climactic enough for the close. In the tried plan, however, each had to take its turn in each of the four quarters of the eight-day session. The problem was to find a way to operate in a straight line instead of in a series of circles. If a given attraction could open every Chautauqua, we could make sure that that attraction was particularly suited for the first day. The same argument held for each succeeding day, and besides we could build for climaxes, for one thing, and co-ordinate, to quite a degree, the intellectual content of our lectures. Besides all of that, I knew that nearly all attractions had a "best" in music, story or speech, and two days appearance required some of the second best.

I wanted one day stands. If I could effect the desired plan, what a benefaction would accrue to our artistic aspirations, and what a blessing conferred to our transportation problems! The automobile was not yet practicable, and if we had no trains we must console ourselves with horses and vehicles to move our people, and, worst of all, their baggage, with all the instruments, costumes, scenery and props. The obstacle in the new plan was the apparent increased cost of employing and moving a considerably larger number of people, when I had, in fact, been spending too much for that purpose. I was so fearful that I was reluctant, at first, to take pencil and paper and figure it all out. When I finally did so, I was surprised to discover that my costs would be less rather than more. Even though I had once been invited to teach mathematics in an academy, I think I must have had but little instinct for calculation that I did not grasp the reason without a pencil. So far as that is concerned no one else had conceived it because all others were doubtful without visual proof. The reason is easily apparent. Some talent cost much more than others, although salary amount did not necessarily indicate program value. If the salary of a "big day" attraction were say $1,750.00 a week, and it were scheduled for two days, the total program expense for a city must include five hundred dollars of that sum, while if it were making a one-day stop, the expense sum would only be two hundred and fifty dollars. On the other hand, the talent for another day might be paid as little as four hundred and fifty dollars a week, and the per diem cost for the town would be sixty-five dollars. Briefly, saving in a one-day stand for the higher-bracket people would permit of the employment of more people, a better variety, and all the other advantages I have mentioned. I figured that travel cost would be no more, and in practice it proved to be less; and while our platform people had to move every day down the long trail, they traveled in greater ease. Thus while in the old plan city number one on the circuit must be no farther than fifty or seventy-five miles from number four, in the new way number four might safely be two hundred and fifty miles or more from number one.

With the platform manager, his crew and tents, however, the case was different. They had to make a long jump, past all the other outfits, and might move five hundred miles or more, but since the circuit often turned to another main line and moved backward, sometimes the jump was short indeed. Anyhow, crew and equipment moves were less important than the travel for talent who had to move every day.

Then there was another point. The long list of lectures produced a rather heavy oratorical fare, too much, perhaps, for proper assimilation. Therefore, I decided to cut to seven days, with a daily change in program. With the prospect of more, and presumably better talent, our committees welcomed the change, and in a seven-day session each could still have a Sunday included. That fact lost some of its value years later, as I will try to show.

I made all of that computation on the train while I was on the way to a conference with Vawter, who, it will be remembered, like me, had suffered a financial loss in 1908. I asked him how he would like to change his program daily, with all the advantages of co-ordination and climaxes. He said it would be an answer to prayer, as he was as sick of second bests as I was. But, he added, it would break us up. When I showed him my figures he was as much surprised as I had been, and he adopted the plan at once. So henceforth, his session was to be increased from six days to seven.

That plan was, I think, my best contribution to the Chautauqua movement. It was the pattern that was closely followed by all the systems that appeared as the years went on, and was followed without change even when the number of Chautauquas had moved far into the thousands.

Notwithstanding my enthusiasm for the new plan, I was in straits. I had no partners nor fellow stockholders. The circuit had to be lengthened to effect economy. I needed some more tents and they had to be manufactured and paid for. New agents had to be found and employed, but, more important, they had to be trained. We had been living in an apartment and, with my second baby, I wanted a home. I found a pleasant place, well located, in Lincoln and bought it at once. I had been corresponding with Mr. John Redmond, the great Irish leader, and, as he was coming to America, I went to Boston to see him. With all my Irish blood I wanted him to make a lecture tour in the United States. I saw him in Boston, and some years later met him again. He told me that he would lecture for me when Ireland got its freedom. He did not live to realize that, and I thought of him with sorrow when I was in Dublin at the time of the first meeting of the Dail of the new State.

But long trips and the purchase of a new home did not lessen my financial burdens. It could not be said that at that stage the Chautauqua was recognized as a sound business, and I had no credit at the banks, but I did have a good name in some of the towns on the circuit in which I borrowed some cash. In the emergency I turned momentarily to real estate. I bought another house and sold it at a profit. I found an attractive area near my new home and built a few cottages which, fortunately, I gainfully sold readily enough. Besides my profit, it was evident that the venture added to the confidence of my agents and they went out with renewed vigor. I covered a larger area in Lyceum bookings, and could expect greater gain from that source. One way and another we got along pretty well, and reached out into Oklahoma and Colorado to lengthen the circuit.

I tried something else, which in pattern turned out to furnish quite an addition to Chautauqua operations. In my territory, for every city financially able to meet the requirements of my circuit, there were several smaller towns, just as good in intelligence and community pride, but with a population too small to undertake the necessary guarantees. So I decided to prepare a Chautauqua of five days, built on smaller scale and yet good and attractive. I selected my old stamping grounds, the part of Nebraska north of the Platte, for a trial. We made contracts with about twenty towns, and as the summer of 1909 brought good weather into September, I was able to operate these with the same tents, by striking out one section to reduce the size. We required an advance sale of only four hundred tickets at a dollar and a half, and the effort was really crowned with success. That is how the five-day Chautauqua appeared, and afterwards all Chautauquas seemed to run for either seven days or five. It was very interesting but too inviting to many other managers, and in time the point of saturation was reached and the decline began. However, this first five-day circuit grew to the length of a season the following year, and it lived for nineteen years.

I named the first circuit the Premier. I thought that in history and plan and quality it had the right to the title. Some who came into the field later might have contested the claim, and certainly their products were as good and maybe even better than mine. But the Premier stood as a standard of a sort for the twenty-two years of its existence. We called the first five-day circuit the Pioneer, and it soon reached from Nebraska into South Dakota, Wyoming, Colorado and northern Kansas.

A year or two after the birth of the Pioneer, we organized the third, or Sterling Circuit. This was cast in a little wider scope than the Pioneer, required an advance sale of seven hundred dollars in season tickets, and covered the States of Kansas, Oklahoma, Arkansas, Texas, Colorado, and New Mexico. At last we produced the fourth, the Star Circuit. It lapped up some of the towns missed by the other three, and others that were fatigued in campaign but did not want to give up. It was a little thinner in talent and I don't think any of us were very proud of it, but it found its place in the general scheme of things.

The Premier grew in dimensions and popularity. By 1917 it reached into twelve states, extended into California, enjoyed a season of twenty continuous weeks and included a hundred and forty cities. It furnished a pleasant road to travel and the glorious scenery and cooler climate of the mountain states provided an agreeable break in the long, hot summer.

Meanwhile we had again incorporated our business into the Redpath-Horner Chautauquas. A few of our best men became stockholders and we had as fine an organization as ever existed. In 1910 I took over a large territory in Lyceum activities and became a director of the Redpath Lyceum Bureau which, under the forceful enterprise of Harry P. Harrison, had bought out its largest competitor, the Slayton Bureau. There were five directors, each with his own territory and at liberty to have as many branch offices as he chose. Each man operated his own business quite independent of the others, made his profits or sustained his losses without affecting directly the others.

Crawford Peffer, the veteran, was in New York and presided over the New England, East Central, and one or two of the South Coast states. W. V. Harrison, a brother of Harry, had his headquarters in Columbus, Ohio, and operated chiefly in Ohio and West Virginia. Harry Harrison was in Chicago with a very large and populous area. Keith Vawter, from Cedar Rapids, contented himself with Minnesota, Iowa and South Dakota. With the development in our operations, I moved to Kansas City, Missouri, and busied myself with Lyceum affairs in Missouri, Arkansas, Oklahoma, Texas, Nebraska, Kansas and Louisiana. I purchased the Central Bureau, my chief Lyceum competitor, and a few years later Keith Vawter and I bought out the Midland Bureau.

Among the five of us, branch offices were maintained, not always continuously, in Boston, Rochester, New York, Pittsburgh, Columbus, Atlanta, Dallas, Lincoln,

Denver, Seattle and Los Angeles. These were for Lyceum purposes, for when Peffer and the Harrisons entered the Chautauqua field each of the five of us maintained a tight supervision over his caravans from his own base city. There was no direct financial advantage to any of us in the organization, for each man had to make all of his own profits and pay all of his losses.

However, there was a fine mutuality in counsel and our buying power was large. Even the talent that had commanded good fees heretofore had not enjoyed decent security in income and length of season, and there was always the dreaded spectre of open or unemployed time. By pooling our needs and responsibilities we could be very brave in making long-time contracts at guaranteed rates. We found that a desirable attraction, working as many weeks in each year as was proper in Lyceum and Chautauqua, would require fourteen years to appear but once in each of our courses, although no one ever tried to do so.

THE ORGANIZATION

Since I have spent forty years in organizational work, City, National and Government, I feel that I can appraise objectively the merits of the Redpath-Horner structure with all its affiliated and subsidiary groups that came into existence. I have never found elsewhere an organization more efficient, competent, alert and devoted as to its component parts. There was no profit-sharing plan, excepting for the interests of a very small number of minority stockholders, and only occasionally any offer of bonuses. There was but little room for profit motive. In proportion to our very large risks, financial gain at the very best never amounted to much. Of all the managers who were active in the field I can think of none who gained a fortune, and only three or four who could retire with a reasonable competence from what he had made. I am sure we should have been more concerned about profit. We talked little of it, and planned more to avoid loss than to gain wealth. That feeling was inherent in the business because if we had not shared in the application of the ideals we were trying to impart and awaken, we would not have made much progress in gaining and retaining public approval. If we had clearly netted 6 per cent of our gross receipts, most of us would have had more money than we ever possessed. Yet all of the systems were formed on a profit basis, excepting one which was underwritten as a .nonprofit institution. Oddly enough, that one was the first and, I think, the only that ended in receivership.

Quite clearly the men and women of the organization, young people for the most part, were in the business for salaries of course, but very positively for the pleasant and inspiring work and excellent training it afforded. It was hard, grueling work, too, the kind that confers happiest memories in days to come. The larger number of our employed attained marked success in their lives and indicates our good fortune in selecting them.

Each circuit had its separate manager with its own list of talent, and its several tents and crews, junior girls, agents and advance men. Over all was a sales manager, the outstanding one being H. H. Kennedy, who became very prominent in the business world. Serving all was an advertising division, routing experts, auditors, talent scouts and coaches and trainers for young talent. Each unit in operation was an outfit, and that would include platform manager, crew, junior girl, the big top and other tents with their heavy load of poles, stakes and ropes, a high and long canvas wall which surrounded the big top, leaving plenty of space for movement and circulating air. Also the outfit must have lighting equipment, tools, extra canvas, advertising, a ticket office, platform decorations, costumes for children's pageants, and many other things. On the Premier Circuit seven outfits were in use each day, but two extra had to be provided, because each must have two days to tear down, jump ahead and set up again.

On that circuit, therefore, there were nine outfits, and seven each for the Sterling, Pioneer and Star circuits. In addition we had reserve tents and sections of them for emergency use in case a tent was damaged by the wind, beyond the repairs the crew could make.

A heavy freight load were the main masts, the quarter poles and side poles for the big top, and those that supported the canvas enclosure. Shipping costs of this weighty property were so high that we found a way to make up quarter, side and wall poles from timbers we could secure in each city and we bought carloads of main poles and stakes and kept a complete set stored in each town on the circuit. In the long run that was less expensive than to ship from place to place. Perhaps some of this property is lying around even yet, unless it has been expropriated for local use. Expert canvasmen were retained, and they were always on the alert to rush into a town to help repair damage or to furnish new tents if necessary. I often wished for an airplane to move about quickly, and was negotiating for one when we got into the big war, and plane sales were stopped.

The plains states enjoy a fine proportion of good weather, but that area is subject to sudden thunderstorms accompanied by high winds. With thirty big tents in the air, I always felt great concern for the public and my people. We trained our tent boys carefully and rehearsed them again and again. If any guy rope showed signs of wear and weakness it was replaced at once. All main ropes were double staked and tightened frequently. We found there was something of an art in spreading canvas properly and setting poles and moorings in the spots determined mathematically. Moreover we would secure a weather committee in each city. The men of it were old-timers accustomed to scanning the skies, and they were on hand to warn us if the weather was too threatening. As a result of our care, we had only a very few accidents in all the years, and scarcely any injuries. We were prepared for any threat of fire, too. We knew that the tents were inflammable because of a treatment administered to the canvas to render it rainproof, and it was the custom to have people on the alert to watch for sparks although we never had a fire. The world shuddered at the fearful conflagration in the big circus in Connecticut. That was something that I, for one, had feared for many years. Actually there was but little danger to life in our case. The sides of our tents were rolled to the top all the time when people were present, unless during rainy weather when there was no danger from fire anyway. With open sides our audience could emerge in a minute or two.

At the peak of our operations, with the need to have available nearly forty big tops, eight miles of enclosing canvas wall and all the accessories, together with storage and repairing facilities, we established a tent factory of our own in Olathe, Kansas. This not only reduced our costs substantially but we could engage in the making of tents and awnings for the trade, and accept some contracts from other Chautauqua systems. Its superintendent was a top-notch canvasman and the enterprise insured the availability of expert assistance in any emergency.

Having suffered for years an unsatisfied yearning for printer's ink, early in 1921 I bought the controlling stock in *The Olathe Register,* a very good little Kansas newspaper. I served as its editor, which provided me one of my many happy experiences in life. Olathe is the seat of Johnson County, which includes a considerable area of Greater Kansas City. It was only eighteen miles from my home in Mission Hills, an admirable suburb of Kansas City, and near enough for frequent visits. I acquired some interest in an Olathe bank, and altogether was again in a position to enjoy some of the rare community fellowship of a small city. Olathe became a very important naval training base during World War II, and is a most interesting and progressive little City.

Ownership of the newspaper brought an important asset to the Redpath-Horner organization. We had a good printing office and sufficient equipment to care for our trade and still assume the heavy load of printing for all of our enterprises. Somehow I could never keep my fingers out of new and untried business ventures. One reason was that on the circuits a number of very capable young men of fine character and ability were developing rapidly and I craved for an opportunity to advance my associations with them. Such a lad was C. R. Churchill, an advance man and agent of sterling worth. He assumed the management of *The Olathe Register* and had special skill among the printing presses. When I was called to Washington at the beginning of the New Deal, he accompanied me as executive assistant and made an enviable reputation for himself. He is now a prominent businessman in Kansas City.

Another and earlier noteworthy chap was J. R. Beach, an Iowa boy attending the University of Nebraska. As a student he worked as a crewman on the circuit and soon showed so much enterprise that he filled many useful places. In 1912, as he was beginning his senior year, I suggested that he prepare himself in office work, in which case I would engage him as my secretary when he received his diploma. Accordingly he applied himself so diligently during the following year that he emerged as a well-trained man, and won his Phi Beta Kappa key at the same time.

Beach had an excellent flair for accounting and administration and an ear for the lure of counting houses. So we bought a few small banks in Kansas and Colorado, one of which he managed and the others he supervised.

There were several other links in our little chain of activities, and with them all there was a large amount of printing to be done. Posters, bills, window cards, catalogues and supplies required numerous millions of pieces of printing, and our shop rolled them all from its presses.

A few pages back I referred to a complaint of some critics of the Chautauqua that the male quartette was the only thing indigenous to it. As a matter of fact I doubt if even that grudging admission is true. The college glee club and the barber shop might dispute such a claim if it were made. I do not know that the Chautauqua actually created anything. However, I believe it conceived some important ideas and proceeded far in the development of certain policies, some of which have been successfully applied in other fields, and all could be used with profit in the business and social structure of the country. Also it developed a cohesive group technique which I believe to be unsurpassed.

Now, I must mention the platform managers. They were an extraordinary lot, young men mostly, but occasionally included a veteran from the local Assembly days. Some were teachers, professors and preachers on leave of absence. Others were lawyers fresh from Law School, and seeking a place to hang their shingles. Also we had a scientist or two, youthful engineers not set in practice, Y. M. C. A. secretaries, athletic coaches, or half-blown authors of books or plays. All had been college men and sought summer pay, adventure and experience. The pay was not enriching, perhaps, from fifty to seventy-five dollars a week. But in adventure and experience they must have achieved their fondest desires. We put them through a rigorous if a short training school, but that would have been of insufficient value if they had not the fine qualities for a most exacting job.

Some of those men were so versatile in talent it is not quite fair to classify them as platform manager alone, although I know of no higher class in the Chautauqua personnel. Take George Aydelott for example. He was an ordained minister. In season he was one of the best booking agents in the field. He was a first-rate manager and sometimes directed the affairs of a circuit. He was a good lecturer and not only could substitute on occasion, but also he could and did fill a season of speaking engagements with credit to himself and his organization. Such a description fits others. Robert Finch was one. Roy Bendell was another. "Army" Ambrose, first a good engineer then a school superintendent, was another. That man served well as a scientific lecturer and later achieved a wide and high reputation in a great industrial concern. Still another, a younger man, was L. E. Moyer, Jr., who joined the movement later in its course. He was a good specimen of a peaceful fighting man. His mettle was sorely tried because the circuits were waning but he did much to revive interest. Later, with Bryan Horner, he succeeded to the management of our Lyceum division and was to achieve an enviable record in Community Chest work.

All of them were capable and some were quite brilliant. They had to be on hand, well groomed and smiling, for every session, however hard they had toiled during the forenoons or far into the night. They were on the platform when the curtain rose, always ready with a bit of chaffing, a funny story, an encomium for the talent to come and a fit introduction for those at hand. It was not safe for the platform manager or any of the talent they extolled to appropriate a bon mot or a story from any of their colleagues. Discipline prevented, and the audience would have resented the plagiary. Instead he must be a watchdog of a sort to see that sparkling yarn and repartee were not borrowed inadvertently from the jewels that fell from the lips of the rightful owner. He learned the town in his short stay, and as he spoke to his audience he would call people by name. He had to be good because he had the guarantee to collect, and, in the most compelling hour, persuade the good citizens to sign the contract for next year. Whatever wit and good humor he expressed were easy and natural. He had no staff to put a new dress on stories oft told before, nor research expert, nor gag writer. If the Chautauqua produced a type for skillful words and bright friendly personality, call it the platform manager. He has descended in kind to the radio, and the master of ceremonies of the stage show and night club from which old-timers listen again to most of the same jokes and stories that rippled in the Chautauqua tents, although his modern version can brazenly use quips and stories of a color the platform manager could not have had the brass to express.

Secondly, I should say, the Chautauqua as an organization developed a concordant spirit, and reciprocal confidence and mutuality of interests and efforts between it and the cities it served. Its personnel had to possess decency and other ample honest values since its very foundations rested on public trust. Sometimes the good citizens had to dig into their pockets to make deficits. It was no easy task to sell all the tickets, and many could ill afford to sacrifice all the time the job required. If they had a deficit it was supplied from their pockets. If, as often, their hard work yielded a profit balance, the amount was saved for another Chautauqua or used in some other worthy community project. In profit or loss, they signed a contract for the next year and signed cheerfully for many years. In a way they were buying a pig in a poke for the manager could not announce his program a year in advance. The committee trusted the manager, who realized that the trust must not be betrayed.

The people would work in zeal for the coming Chautauqua. Often they would unite to cut the weeds, mow the grass, trim the trees, decorate the windows and even paint some buildings so that the town would be neat and handsome for the inspection of visitors. Many businessmen would organize booster trips to visit the countryside and neighbor towns to advertise the coming event, and to promise a welcome to prospective guests from far and near. Preachers would often make the Chautauqua a subject for their sermons in advance, and Sunday evening services and midweek prayer meetings were usually cancelled or held at an early hour so that their congregations could feel free to go to the tent. Strange to relate, many stores and other business houses would lock their doors during the afternoon and evening program hours. The mothers would bake and cook in advance, and freely welcome to their homes the itinerant Chautauquans. The long hot trail blossomed with a never-ending series of good cheer plentifully embellished with fried chicken.

The platform manager, crew and junior girl were adopted and feasted for the week. The generous ladies of the town would bring flowers in abundance to the tent, and flags, rugs, lamps and other decorations for the platform. Farmers would stop to leave fruit and watermelons, and so many picnics were arranged that I often wondered how the hard-pressed crewmen could perform all their tasks. If inspiration and good will flowed from the platform, they swelled to a flood in the spirit of harmony that prevailed during the week. Once, at least, during the year, a spirit of harmony ruled the town and often did we hear these words spoken by the Committee: "If only we could all work together throughout the year as we do for the Chautauqua, what a city this would be."

There is ample evidence that this aggressive good feeling bore tangible fruit. For example, the fervent junior girl, as she herded her flocks of children to some sheltered spot for play, story hour or pageant practice, might discover a desirable incipient parklet or tree-grown vacant block. Or perhaps a park, which, like the old-fashioned parlor, had been retained for pride rather than use, or, sadly, she might find nothing of the kind. In any event the need of a playground was often dramatized. The junior girl, being a trained play supervisor, and bold to express her opinions, missed no opportunity to urge community leaders to provide space and equipment for the permanent use of her flock. Moreover, in co-operation with the American Recreation Association, we often borrowed from the staff of that worthy institution, and added an expert in supervised play and community self-entertainment. He would deliver his lecture from the platform, and afterwards confer with forward-looking men and women, and as a result of it all many parks and fields for games would blossom along the Chautauqua trail.

Our contract with a committee was identical with the ones made with all the others. The terms were simply and plainly written and confined to a few printed lines. The committee agreed to sell and pay for a certain number of season tickets, furnish the ground, and the lumber for seats and platform. All the other fine service the men rendered was voluntary. They shared in the receipts of season tickets over the initial guarantee, and got a share of the money from single admissions. Our costs were considerably more in amount than the proceeds of the guarantee, and we had to look to oversales and single admissions for the balance of the expense, and for profit. Contracts used by other systems were the same in form and nearly identical in terms, although the amount of guarantee was variable. They were noble men and women, those people of the committee, and I doubt if the nation has ever seen a truer example of community unity and unselfishness.

The newspapers furnished strength to both committee and managers. They made news of the Chautauqua and were generous with space. They would make up whole pages in advertising with the Chautauqua for a theme. We took all the advertising space we could afford. Advertising copy was mailed to the newsmen from our central office and we always attached a check to each piece of copy, and never bothered to check the printing because we knew we always received more room in the columns than we could possibly pay for. As a matter of fact every expense was paid promptly in cash, and when we could, we paid in advance.

The stage has an admirable and courageous tradition that "the show must go on." Scarcely less than death itself could prevent a bruised or stricken actor from marching through his lines. Our talent had a similar ideal. Not alone must they give their performance, but hungry, sleepy and fatigued, come high water or delayed trains, they somehow must get to the next town. Many a time must the brave people go on to the platform with smiling faces, although they had not been in bed for twenty-four hours, or longer. No doubt the summer-long journey with its work in the open air was healthful, but if there was sickness it must not interfere with the date. However, a lecturer would double back for extra duty to relieve a sick brother and then ride all night to get back to his place.

One night in the early summer of 1913 the talent went to bed for a good rest in Commerce, Texas, since they could take a late forenoon train to Greenville, only a few miles away. A terrific rainstorm flooded the city, and the alert platform manager, long after midnight, found that the rails were covered and no trains could run. He had to awaken his talent before daylight, and as soon as it was light enough to see, he loaded them into buggies for the journey. Fortunately, it was a small group of six people, and I happened to be along. There was, happily, only one lady in the group. The roads were inundated and rain fell unceasingly. That was before the era of good highways. One road after another was closed because bridges were gone. When we finally came to water too deep for our vehicles, we constructed rafts of a sort, or maybe found a boat. The men of the company could always carry their prima donna from cart to buggy to lumber wagon and manage to keep her out of the flood. When we had to abandon one means of transportation and cross a stream, we would find a farmer with wagon and mules and proceed until stopped again. The distance we traveled was three times what it would have been if we had gone direct. At the last we came to a railroad which was above water and found hand cars which the Greenville people had sent out. So we pumped triumphantly the last six miles and arrived at the tent after dark to find an audience waiting.

We had been fifteen hours on the way, and all of us but the favored one were wet and muddy to our waists. There was time for neither food nor change of garments, but our talent went on and gave both the afternoon and evening programs in one, and no one seemed to be regretful or the worse for the adventure. Mr. Frank J. Cannon, who had been the first United States Senator from Utah when that state was admitted to the Union, was the moving spirit of the damp journey. He would prod the others to action when their spirits flagged. He would belabour the mules that momentarily were pulling us while the other men would tug at the wheels. He would shout encouragement when younger men would strip to their underclothes to swim and convey a raft of sorts. "We can always go another inch," he would say when we paused for rest; "and when we have made that we will be good for another one." Yet, his clothing covered with mud, when he finally began his lecture, he was as calm as if he had walked only from his hotel.

That is only one of many tales of heroism that might be told of the talent, and I happened to be a witness to that. To be sure the travel was not always difficult, and often it was easy indeed, but it had to be undertaken each day, and each man or woman had to sleep in a new bed each night, if indeed he slept at all.

Finally, in considering a type of originality in the organization, I can do no better than to write about the crews. To man as many as thirty outfits required, first and last, a tidy number of young men. They were recruited from the colleges and universities and thousands were available from whom we could choose the ones we wanted. Written applications with necessary information were required, and studied when received. We tried to spread our selections in as many institutions as possible. On a scheduled day it was likely that a good personnel man could proceed to a convenient place and interview fifty or a hundred lads. A good man, who had been tried, could be depended upon for accurate information of a brother collegian, and that simplified the task of choice. While we drew from the large universities, I am of the opinion that some of the small denominational colleges supplied a disproportionate share of the men selected. I do not mean to say that men selected from the small school were better than the ones recruited from the university, but considering the total number of applicants, on an average, those from the denominational college graded higher for our purposes.

By far, a majority of the men were self-dependent, working to pay the expenses of their education. The larger percentage of them did not smoke, and I doubt if ten per cent of them had tasted alcohol, although abstinence in these things was not stated as a necessary qualification. Their homes were in the villages and cities of our area and of course the boys knew well the kind of people who were our public. They had to be educated, intelligent and physically fit for there was much labor for muscles.

When selections were made, the men were given a manual of instructions which they must learn. There were but few rules, if any, of personal conduct, and few of any kind other than those necessary in the care of equipment and protection of the public. They were carefully drilled in the routine of erecting and anchoring the tent, and prizes were awarded to the crews that maintained the best "set-ups" for the season. Even now, after twenty or thirty years, some of the men, grown middle-aged and prosperous, will display a good set-up medal with great pride. The labor was as tough as that of the woodman felling trees in the forest. It was hard on them in the first city. However sturdy their arms and legs, they had aching backs and blistered and bleeding hands to show at first until they became hard and calloused for the long season. They had no eight-hour day, nor regularity in hours of service, because no one could foretell when an emergency might arise. Their home was the Chautauqua tent and they found their meals in the house of some neighboring housewife who usually feasted them well. They had two days between set-ups, but however short or long the intervening distance they knew they had a full night of labor to get their tent into the air and everything in shipshape for the first audience. They had another all-night job to strike the tent, pack up and be on their way at the end of the session. We had no machine to sink the stakes into the sullen earth, and that had to be done by force of sledge hammer and strong arms. If the rain fell and the winds pulled the stakes and billowed the canvas, they had even more to do. Dusty, muddy or wet, they somehow managed to be at their posts, bathed, shaven and freshly dressed, when the people came to the gates.

Warren G. Harding perceived the value in the boys perhaps before other observers did. He wrote to me in 1908 from Sabetha, Kansas, where his lot was cast for a day, "These crewmen strike one as a worth-while lot," he said. He told me that they were our chief asset, and that was a fact.

In many ways there was more glamour in the crew boys than in the beauties of concert companies, the moving lecturer, or even in the platform manager. The people of the town took them into their hearts because they were the same kind of lads as the best they had at home, and many a wayward and lazy local youth was inspired to polish up his own dormant ambition and take a turn at college himself.

The boys had time and opportunity for pleasure along the way, for often in lazy forenoons and calm nights they could go for a swim or a post program party.

They were studious and industrious in their spare time. Instead of cards and dice, there were likely to be found textbooks and manuscripts in their kit bags and trunks. Many had college work to make up because of examinations missed when farsighted deans had permitted them to leave the academic halls before the term was ended. Some were writing papers and theses, and occasionally one would add a page or two to a dissertation he was preparing for his doctorate.

Most people marvel at the efficiency and organizational skill of a great American circus, which with its hundreds of people and trainloads of properties and animals move about all over the nation and give a performance every afternoon and night. I share in a common admiration for such a truly American Institution. However, the Chautauqua organization was not unworthy of praise. Except for the advance men and a few others, the high command of a circus has all of its people and numerous component parts all together, and constantly under its eye. The units of the Redpath-Horner Chautauquas were scattered over many states, and the extreme points were fifteen hundred miles from base. Twenty-two distinct groups of talent must move and perform on schedule. Each advance man and agent had to be in his town at the appointed time. A single outfit of tents, crew and platform manager, was very small compared to the giant circus, but there were thirty of them and each must serve and move in precision. There could be no complete means for supervision or accounting. Redpath-Horner, and the other systems were far-flung organizations but they could not have functioned, if their men had not been intelligent, loyal and dependable. The crews were of the essence of the machine and the platform managers the spark plugs.

Oddly enough, the most heartening, if not sublime, story that I can tell of the crews is based on the misdemeanors of a few of them. The boys were inherently honest. Most of them were poor in pocket and a good stream of cash would flow from the box office through their hands. I thought deeply of the fallacious belief of some high-minded theorists, that young people should be shielded from temptation, that they should be safeguarded from any opportunity to be dishonest. That, of course, is a misconception of character. We decided very early that a basic policy of operations had to be a complete trust in our men. The idea of using spotters or spies was repugnant and wholly contrary to such a policy. If the boys wanted to slip some of our cash into their own pockets, they could do so, and no practiced system of auditing could have prevented it, even if we could have employed it. We even told the lads how they could steal if they would, although they were quite able to see for themselves. When a stream of people were crowding through the gates and there was a line before the ticket office fifty feet or more away, the gatekeeper need only palm some of the tickets, hide them away and find some way to return them to the ticket seller to sell again at once. Then the two could split the "take." It meant that two boys, or possibly a boy and girl, for occasionally the junior girl would sell the tickets, must work in collusion, and each must share the troubled conscience of the other.

It was a frightful thing to contemplate, not because of loss of cash, but it would gnaw at the cornerstone of the foundation of what we had built. Nevertheless we tried to leave no doubts in their minds that we reposed complete trust in their integrity. We knew that there was petty embezzlement but I was troubled less than others because I had stolen twenty-five cents from my father's purse when I was a small boy and suffered enough agony to overbalance what joy one could find in possessing a fortune.

It was during the war and the impact of the laxity of morals of the early days following that we knew the little defalcations might become a matter of serious concern. One of our vice-presidents at the time was Charles Mayne, a noble soul who had gained a good reputation as a leading General Secretary in the Y. M. C. A. Mayne took the matter very much to heart and had an unerring instinct to sense little lapses in behavior. His wise counsel and friendly sympathy and understanding did more to alleviate the trouble than any mode of punishment anyone could devise. In due time evidence came to me that was quite sufficient to send a few lads to jail, and some of our advisers felt that some of them should be brought to book as a wholesome example of others. But nothing of the kind was ever done.

If that were the end of the story it would be a sordid tale. I am still convinced that we acted wisely and in our own interest as well as that of the boys. I, of course, had no means of knowing how much of our cash found an unlawful place in the pockets of the crews. I am certain that it was not much; a few hundreds, perhaps, maybe a few thousands over a period of twenty years, and I suspect most of it came back to me in the end, in a way that proved a good man's conscience is his best judge and jury. We were dealing with good men.

Letters began to come to me. Contrite letters from shame-hearted boys and girls. One day, years later, I was having lunch in Washington with a gentleman who was a high executive in a great industry, national in character, with branches in many cities. For years he had extended favors to me that no man could reasonably expect from another. I told him I was a little embarrassed because of his unusual kindness and that I could never expect to repay him in kind.

He told me that he was only paying a debt that was thirty years old, and that the last installment must be a confession. He had been a crew boy, many years ago. He was working his way through college and needed money so much he had taken forty dollars, in small amounts at a time, through a summer period. He had been trying to pay in kindness the interest on the debt, he said, and now that he had finally owned up, he felt better and invited me to take what reprisal I would.

He was not the only one who told me a similar story face to face, but most of the confessions were in letters. Many of them were not delayed so long, and some were written soon after the errors. The last

I received only a short time ago. It was written by a man who stood high in his chosen profession and had become as wealthy as he was successful. He had his little shortages figured out to a penny, added interest to the amount and sent me a check for the sum. He said he did not ask me to hold the matter in confidence, and that he would cheerfully accept any damage to his reputation that could come from publicity. One other letter, with a remittance, also late to arrive, was written by a missionary in South Africa. A few wrote to me from the battlefields in Europe during the war, and the most touching of all was from a lad whose words expressed so much true nobility of manhood, I wish I might read it again. He said he had arranged to have some one in America repay the amount he had taken. The check came to me not long afterwards, but I never saw the lad again because he was one of those who had been buried under the little white crosses in France.

Altogether I received perhaps fifty such letters, which I feel must have accounted for nearly all of the precious culprits. Not one of them asked for secrecy, all pleaded for forgiveness and the letters were manly and forthright in tone. While they differed, as men will differ, in words of atonement, there was one statement common, I think, to them all. They said that what impressed them most in our service was the fact that we had trusted them and because of that confidence they must make the restitution, and that after thus clearing their troubled minds they believed they would never again be unworthy of trust. I reread all of the letters some ten years ago when I took them from an iron box to which no one had access but myself. So far as I know, no other eyes than mine ever saw the letters after they were received, and none will because I destroyed them all. I think a reawakened sense of honor in the boys was of greater value to them, to me, and to the world, than a prison sentence.

Those crew boys had the stuff and sinews of good Americans, I think I could say great Americans. As I have visited many cities all over the nation throughout the years gone by, if my presence was known, some one or more of them would come to see me, and it was seldom, indeed, that I did not discover that they were high and strong in the affairs of the city and successful in their business or profession. I would like to call a roll of those fellows today, and to know how and where they stand in the movement of life. Those I know most about have lived a strong life. Perhaps some of the others failed, but I don't know of any such. If I see some of them again, and wherever they may be, I would expect them to be stalwart citizens, leading in community affairs, for Chautauqua people are not likely to forget that their own community is their part of America, and that the whole nation is a great family of neighborhoods.

THE SYSTEMS MULTIPLY

Meanwhile the grand old independent Chautauquas were having their troubles. They had been the source for inspiration for the early managers. We respected, and almost held them in reverence. But no longer did they have a goodly part of a whole state to themselves. When the automobile succeeded the horse and buggy, local travelers did not care so much for week-end excursions on the trains. The single city could not possibly operate so economically as the system and moreover the tried and true talent preferred the security and better net pay offered by the circuit. But the currents that flowed from their tent cities surely traced the way for a great movement. Some of us never forgot our debt of gratitude, and we tried to assist, by doubling in for them some of our speakers, when we could. Gradually many of them came to circuits and others ceased to be.

Keith Vawter and I did not have the field to ourselves very long. Within two or three years other Lyceum managers began to make Chautaqua plans for themselves, and within ten years other numerous astute managers cast in their lines. I am parading no magnanimity of spirit nor self-abnegation when I say we welcomed them and gave what assistance we could in counsel, when it was sought. I have no doubt we were sure of ourselves, and perhaps vain, and felt that no others could adumbrate or even approach our own growing enterprise. We invited them to visit our circuits, examine our plans and learn all they could. I must confess there was a more or less tacit hope that the new men would find other fields than in the states we had staked out, and at first that was what happened. Three other Redpath managers began to build tents and hire crews. They, of course, were in our own managerial family and there was ample room for us all.

Harry P. Harrison, as could have been expected, entered the arena with ardor and sweeping plans that almost at once placed him in the front ranks. He enjoyed a substantial advantage in getting into Florida and other southern states before any one else. With the warm climate there he could open his great circuit in March and thus build for the longest season of all. From Florida he could move northward through the central states to Wisconsin and Illinois. Vernon Harrison confined himself to a smaller but more densely populated area and operated two circuits in Ohio, West Virginia and Pennsylvania. Crawford Peffer spread his canvas in New York and New England. Coit and Alber, two excellent Lyceum Bureau managers, organized a circuit from Cleveland, Ohio. Sam Holliday headquartered in Des Moines, Iowa, and a boyhood friend of mine from Lexington, Nebraska, moved to Lincoln and established the Standard Chautauquas. White and Meyers, later White and Brown, blossomed out from my own center of operations,

Kansas City, Missouri.   Benjamin Franklin settled himself in Topeka, Kansas.   Two brilliant brothers produced the Community System in Indiana, and the Mutual Lyceum Bureau, of Chicago, with Frank Morgan at the head, added a circuit to their activities.

Out in the Northwest, J. R. Ellison, an old Redpath man, joined with C. H. White and cut a great dash in that area, which they had pretty much to themselves as they kept an eye on their chains of tents from Portland and Boise City.   They were very daring and perhaps more adventurous than any of us because they sailed with their personnel and equipment to far off Australia and New Zealand and introduced our type of thought and entertainment to the people in the Antipodes.   In Canada an American lad named J. M. Erickson, who has been around the tents a great deal, covered quite all of the south part of the Dominion from Toronto to Vancouver.

An old schoolman, Mr. W. S. Rupe, was one of the last to exercise managerial hands.   Certainly he was one of the last to strike his tents for the last time.   His bravery approached audacity.   He would buy a circuit here and a part of one there until he was likely to be found in almost any part of the country.   Two other men, Jones of Iowa and Radcliff from Washington, D. C., contented themselves with three-day programs, both covering a wide expanse of territory.

Paul Pearson, a professor in Swarthmore College in Philadelphia, and a lecturer of high standing, chose his time of entry carefully, and made all possible thoughtful preparation before he bought his tents. He was wise enough to avoid some mistakes of the early days, and he was well organized as the Swarthmore Chautauquas from the beginning. Dr. Pearson was a conspicuous figure in the movement. He brought back a positive educational flavor, which, I fear, some systems had not heeded so much.

In the years 1919, 1920 and 1921 I served as director of a bureau for statistical research for the International Lyceum and Chautauqua Association. I was ably assisted by Dr. Paul Pearson and Mr. George Whitehead. Personally I spent much time and effort in acquiring and compiling information concerning the Lyceum and Chautauqua. My report was completed and published in September 1921. So far as I know, that report contains the only definite and accurate information concerning the numerical scope of the movement.

It was a pleasant task although I spent an aggregate of several months on the job. Most of the managers were as frank and honest in revealing their figures as though I had belonged to their organizations instead of a competing one. Their co-operation was characteristic of the mutual faith we all felt in each other.

I found that in 1920 there were twenty-one companies operating Chautauquas and forty-one that were booking Lyceum courses.

Following is a list of both. There are, of course duplicates in the lists; that is, some companies belong to both categories:

CHAUTAUQUA

Acme Chautauquas, Des Moines, Iowa
Chautauqua Association of Pennsylvania, Swarthmore, Pennsylvania
Community Chautauquas, Greencastle, Indiana
Community Chautauquas, New Haven, Connecticut
Coit & Alber Chautauquas, Cleveland, Ohio
Cadmean Chautauquas, Topeka, Kansas
Ellison-White and Dominion Chautauquas, Portland, Oregon
Jones Chautauqua System, Perry, Iowa
Midland Chautauquas, Des Moines, Iowa
Mutual Chautauquas, Chicago, Illinois
Redpath Chautauquas, White Plains, New York
Redpath Chautauquas, Columbus, Ohio
Redpath-Vawter Chautauquas, Cedar Rapids, Iowa
Redpath Chautauquas, Chicago, Illinois
Redpath-Horner Chautauquas, Kansas City, Missouri
Radcliff Chautauqua System, Washington, D. C.
Independent-Cooperative Chautauqua, Bloomington, Illinois
Standard Chautauqua System, Lincoln, Nebraska
Travers-Newton, Des Moines, Iowa
White & Myers Chautauquas, Kansas City, Missouri
International Chautauquas, Bloomington, Illinois

LYCEUM

Alkhahest Lyceum System, Atlanta, Georgia
Antrim Lyceum Bureau, Philadelphia, Pennsylvania

Brown Lyceum Bureau, St. Louis, Missouri
Coit-Alber Dominion Lyceum Bureau, Toronto,
  Ontario
Columbia Lyceum Bureau, Salina, Kansas
Community Lyceum Bureau, Aurora, Missouri
Ellison-White Lyceum Bureau, Portland, Oregon
United Lyceum Bureau, Columbia, Ohio
Dennis Lyceum Bureau, Wabash, Indiana
Kansas Lyceum Bureau, Lyndon, Kansas
Inter-State Lyceum Bureau, Chicago, Illinois
Midland Lyceum Bureau, Des Moines, Iowa
Mutual Lyceum Bureau, Chicago, Illinois
National Alliance, Cincinnati, Ohio
Redpath Lyceum Bureau, White Plains, New York
Redpath Lyceum Bureau, Columbus, Ohio
Redpath Lyceum Bureau, Chicago, Illinois
Redpath-Vawter, Cedar Rapids, Iowa
Redpath-Horner Lyceum Bureau, Kansas City,
  Missouri
Redpath Lyceum Bureau, Dallas, Texas
Redpath Lyceum Bureau, Birmingham, Alabama
Redpath Lyceum Bureau, Denver, Colorado
Redpath Lyceum Bureau, Pittsburgh, Pennsylvania
Royal Lyceum Bureau, Syracuse, New York
Standard Lyceum Bureau, Lincoln, Nebraska
White Entertainment Bureau, Boston, Massachusetts
White & Myers, Kansas City, Missouri
Dominion Lyceum Bureau, Calgary, Canada
Allen Lyceum Bureau, Lima, Ohio
Century Lyceum Bureau, Chicago, Illinois
Coit-Alber Lyceum Bureau, Boston, Massachusetts

Coit-Neilsen Lyceum Bureau, Pittsburgh, Pennsylvania

Continental Lyceum Bureau, Louisburg, Kentucky

Cooperative Lyceum Bureau, Sullivan, Illinois

Dixie Lyceum Bureau, Dallas, Texas

Edwards Lyceum Bureau, Grand Cane, Louisiana

Piedmont Lyceum Bureau, Asheville, North Carolina

Emerson Lyceum Bureau, Chicago, Illinois

Chicago Circuit Lyceum Bureau, Chicago, Illinois

Western Lyceum Bureau, Waterloo, Iowa

In 1920 the Chautauqua Companies operated ninety-three circuits in the United States and Canada. These circuits included eight thousand five hundred eighty towns and cities. The gross attendance aggregated 35,449,750 people. Some of the circuits were quite small and some operated as few as three days in a town.

Our studies continued quite late in the season of 1921, and while the figures obtained for that year were not entirely accurate I can say, conservatively, that the total number of Chautauquas increased to nine thousand five hundred and ninety-seven operated in nearly a hundred circuits. If the proportionate attendance prevailed, about forty million people passed through the Chautauqua gates. It is possible, however, that attendance per town was a little less than in 1920, because business conditions were not so good in 1921.

Our figures for the Lyceum are not quite so nearly accurate because we had no direct communication with all the towns. Yet they are substantially correct. In the season of 1920-21 (winter season), there were eight thousand seven hundred ninety-five Lyceum or lecture courses which attracted an aggregate attendance of 16,262,649 people, making a gross attendance for both institutions of 56,173,591.

The interrelations of the systems were agreeable. We had a Lyceum and Chautauqua Manager's Association, in which nearly all managers held membership. Frequent meetings were held and all discussed their plans and problems with freedom. There were no trade agreements, but instead a well-recognized code of ethics. We visited the tents of each other and were willing to lend our canvas if that of one of the other blew away. Each spoke well of the others and no one would solicit a future contract in a town currently being served by another. Personally nearly all of us were devoted friends and in our relations and meetings and thoughts were a sense of comradeship not excelled in any other group I have known.

The First World War gave new impetus to the Chautauqua, and during that and the four following years the movement reached its peak. Our people were unprepared in spirit for the war and were perplexed and troubled in mind. All this called out an even more avid interest in public affairs. Many of our good men went into service, and I, for one, had but an occasional fleeting glance or two at my tents in 1917 and 1918. I spent most of the time during the war in Washington where I was a member of the three-man committee for the Liberty Loans, and I directed the speaking activities of the campaign for W. G. McAdoo, Secretary of the Treasury. But, if the war brought new problems to us, it also furnished our best opportunity for service. To the everlasting credit of the Lyceum and Chautauqua it can be clearly shown that all of us were organized and willing to do our part.

My wife and I were enjoying a vacation in Cuba in January, 1917, when the German Kaiser threw off all restraint and announced his policy of unrestricted submarine war. Because of the part I had played in the two Presidential Campaigns for Woodrow Wilson, and from frequent contacts with numerous officials of his administration, there was no doubt in my mind that our days of peace were numbered. We hurried home for there was much to do, and of course I wanted to be ready should I have an opportunity to serve. We were in the midst of a very large Lyceum-selling campaign, the Horner Institute of Fine Arts needed new members in its faculty, and I had undertaken certain local civic obligations. Fortunately, we were well staffed and the circuits were in good order. The Premier was scheduled to open in California early in April, but we were ready for that. We had engaged a special train on the Rock Island and Southern Pacific and all of our people were on board at the appointed time. It was a good train with its lounge and club cars, dining cars, pullmans, enough for everyone, and five baggage cars. It was a pleasant journey and each one had an opportunity to become acquainted with all the others although we knew that such sumptuous travel comforts would end with the raising of the first curtain. Everyone was happy, and as the railroad officials were kind, and enjoying themselves as much as anyone,

we stopped one afternoon at a siding on the sand wastes
of New Mexico. We all landed and our people gave
a grand concert with no audience but ourselves and
some stray Mexicans, who must have been surprised.
When we arrived at El Paso, I received several telegrams, most of them urging me to go to Washington
at once. I was asked to appear before the Senate
Finance Committee to give some testimony in the
pending Revenue Bill. Some messages were from colleagues who wanted me to be there and others from
friends in the Capital, suggesting service I might
render.

I had reason to be grateful for the courtesy of the
railroad men. Some of the telegrams should have a
reply at once, and I was not ready to leave my flock
at a moment's notice. The good people held our train
for forty-five minutes or so while I could get through
some telephone calls. In the end, I finished the journey
on to the Golden State, remained there two days, then
went to Washington. I was met there by Harry P.
Harrison, Keith Vawter, Louis Alber, and perhaps
other managers.

During the summer, Chautauqua lecturers were to
speak to millions of people. We knew the temper and
patriotism of talent and managers and that they could
be depended upon for any service that would be valuable to the government. For one thing Mr. Harrison
had already accepted the chairmanship of a Speaker's
Bureau for the Red Cross and he invited me, with
others of our colleagues, to form the committee.

My appearance before the Senate Finance Committee was interesting enough, although I was grilled a bit by Senator Boies Penrose, whose virile ability impressed me, and Senator Stone of Missouri, whose sarcasm bit rather deeply. Chairman Simmons was a gentle but just and forceful statesman, John Sharp Williams, as brilliant a man as ever sat in the Senate, was very kind, and Senators Gore of Oklahoma and the elder Lafollette of Wisconsin, both of whom had traveled our circuits, furnished all the solace I needed to ease the skin the others had chafed. Incidently, Lyceum and Chautauqua tickets were finally ruled to be exempt from tax because of the educational character of the programs.

We made some plans at once, and I agreed to keep an eye on things. I spent much of the summer in Washington and was able to offer the services of the combined Chautauquas to the Treasury when it was ready to float the first Liberty Loan. President Wilson appreciated the wide and direct channels for information which the platform commanded, and he declared that the Lyceum and Chautauqua were an integral part of the National Defense. I was president of the National Lyceum and Chautauqua Manager's Association at that time and am competent to testify that all managers forgot lines of competition, began at once to adapt their programs to the needs of the war and expended their time and money freely for the purpose.

The talent came forward in a surge. As soon as information lines could be clearly laid, Mr. Montraville Flowers, a great Shakespearian scholar and lecturer,

who was the president of the International Lyceum
and Chautauqua Association, arranged a conference of
platform speakers in Washington which was attended
by hundreds from all parts of the country. Mr. Hoover
told them of the work of the Food Administration,
the Treasury, the War and Navy Departments, and
other divisions sent high officials to explain their work
and reveal what manner of public co-operation was
desired. All who attended the conference paid their
own expenses, or they were paid by the managers, and
a great tide of information and exhortation was carried
to the ears of millions. So far as I know, none of it
cost the Government a penny. Through bulletins and
word of mouth the two Associations kept the whole
Chautauqua and Lyceum vocal army well informed
while the war continued, and the Government needs
formed a major share in the discussions of all circuit
meetings. Early in 1918, a well selected group of
lecturers were brought to Washington. They were
men whose words carried weight among their fellows.
They were sent to the battlefields of Europe under the
direction of the Red Cross, and when they returned,
almost with the scent of powder in their clothes, they
were distributed among the various systems to tell
their story to their colleagues and to the public.

I cannot tell of all the individual efforts made by
managers, and I seek to write only of things that
passed before my eyes. I advertised a contest among
the boys and girls of Redpath-Horner Circuits, and
offered many cash prizes, ranging from a dollar to
seventy-five dollars, for essays on the subject, "What

I can do to help win the war." Schoolteachers or committees were asked to select the best and send them to us for judgment. There must have been a large number written because some five thousand of the best ones that were selected came to us. Awards were made according to the opinion of some nationally known judges, and all of us were amazed with the understanding and patriotism of the youngsters. After reading many of these literary contributions, the wise Governor Hoch of Kansas wrote me that one need never try to tell him that the young generation is a decadent lot.

One other incident indicates the good repute of the platform and the patriotic spirit of the people. I found three lecturers who were both eloquent and full of knowledge concerning the war. They agreed to make a tour of ten weeks at a modest salary with their expenses paid by us. I asked H. H. Kennedy, our forthright sales manager to book these men, one of whom was a veteran from the American or British Army, in sixty towns for a price which would cover only the cost. The project was so popular that instead of sixty towns, he booked the course in several hundred places and I had to find several groups to keep the engagements. The thing went so well and the selling expense was so low, that Kennedy found considerable profit in spite of our patriotic and unselfish plans, although we found a good use for the cash in war work.

I do not think, of course, that the Chautauqua people deserve higher praise than should be accorded to other civilian groups. From my post in the Treasury in Washington, I could mark the tide of unity and will to serve that swept the country. All men were accepting war's restrictions without complaint. I think there was a more positive feeling of individual and community responsibility than existed in the second war because so large a share of the people's solicitude in public matters had not yet been yielded to the Government. Certainly Americans of the second great war were as patriotic and sternminded and determined as they were in 1917 and 1918. And they carried a heavier load in production and military service, but otherwise more of the duties on the home front were assigned to governmental employees.

I wish only to show that the Chautauqua and Lyceum were a powerful and moving force, possibly the greatest in civilian ranks. They were well organized and ready without delay to mobilize public opinion and they had a large and ardent public to listen to and heed what they had to say. I cannot escape the feeling that the custom and temper of the times, the habit of community co-operation and responsibility in 1917 and 1918, served well to augment Government Agencies which were microscopic in personnel compared to those in the 1940s.

WILLIAM JENNINGS BRYAN

From the time when I was a twelve-year-old ranch boy, with an eye eager to catch a glimpse of the world beyond the pastures, I admired and revered Mr. Bryan. He was a real and glowing figure in the turbination of my boyish dreams. When he was elected to Congress from the first Nebraska district, when he made his unsuccessful campaign for the Senate against John M. Thurston, I read all the newspaper stories of his speeches that I could find. His "Cross of Gold" address that swept the Chicago convention in 1896 and placed him in full view of the eyes of the world, fastened itself less securely in my thoughts than my own mental picture of a handsome and fearless knight from the West who strode into the turbulent arena of political conflict, depending solely upon his own strength. His sword was shining words and his shield an invincible faith that he was right.

While I was living in Lincoln, Nebraska, and had made headway with my Chautauqua Circuits, I telephoned Mr. Bryan one day to ask for an appointment. He answered the phone himself. I told him I would like to see him. He didn't inquire why but said to come any time, at once if I cared to. It was not long after his third presidential race, when he was defeated by William Howard Taft. I found an electric suburban car at once and rode to Fairview, which was the name of his home. He had erected a commodious brick house on a high spot on his farm. He often enjoyed himself among his cattle and hogs. He liked to watch the latter as they grunted along their plodding way. They were peaceful creatures, he said, and never made trouble or noise so long as they were well fed.

Since I can never abstain from speaking of cattle, I might as well relate a little amusing story of his. When there were differences in honest opinion between men, Bryan always advocated that matters be approached in the spirit of compromise, although one who yielded too much might not win in the process. He said that when he bought his farm and decided to have some cattle, he and Mrs. Bryan did not favor the same breed. But they had decided to confine themselves to one kind. He wanted Shorthorns, while Mrs. Bryan held out for Jerseys. As they couldn't agree, he proposed that they compromise in the choice. So that is what they did and stocked the farm with Jerseys.

Mr. Bryan answered my ring of the doorbell and led me into his library, which was lined with books and stacks of newspapers and magazines and many articles he had collected in his wide travels over the world. From that day, for many years, I had the privilege occasionally to visit the Bryan home in Lincoln, Washington or Florida. I have never found a more restful and gracious place. The rooms would please the eye of a good housekeeper and a home lover of taste. They were well furnished, in good order and every object in them seemed to be there for comfort and pleasure. Mrs. Bryan was a lady of charm and wit. She was highly educated and when her distinguished husband chose the law as his profession, she acquired a legal education for herself and was admitted to the bar. She possessed an easy, graceful skill as a hostess, and her house never failed to reflect the peace and refinement of their lives.

Mr. Bryan treated me with the same kindly courtesy he accorded to everyone. In this, my first visit, he talked with a candor as clear as anyone could employ after years of secure acquaintance with his listeners. I told him that while I had not been a manager many years, I thought my places were well organized and I would like to have him address some of them. Moreover my associate, Keith Vawter, had many interesting cities under management and I spoke for him as well. He thought the matter might be arranged. He told me that he enjoyed the Chautauquas because they furnished the kind of audience he liked. He had two motives. He desired to express his ideas outside of politics and, as there was ample opportunity for political talks elsewhere, he could leave that field when he accepted platform engagements. His other motive was to make a living and the lecture platform could supply the opportunity. He explained that he would not speak for pay in his home state of Nebraska, and that was a policy he held to so long as he resided there. He believed that Nebraska people saw quite enough of him during the state political campaigns, although when he had moved to Florida to live and the embargo was lifted from Nebraska, I found that he was received quite as well there as in any other part of the nation.

He telephoned to his brother, Charles W. Bryan, told him about me and my desire, and asked him to favor me if he could. When I was ready to go he went to the door with me but I had not gone far until he recalled me to give me a bundle of letters to post in the city. This time he walked along to point out some of the interesting spots about the neighborhood. He parted with me with a handclasp that I always thought held more warmth than that of any one else, but first he said a complimentary word or two which sent me away in a glow. It was an important day in my life for it marked the beginning of a friendship that entwined itself through the fibre of my spirit and became deeply rooted in my life.

I went to see Charles Bryan the next day. He received me as cordially as I had been greeted by his famous brother. He was the publisher and manager of *The Commoner,* a magazine founded and edited by W. J. It had a very large circulation at the time, and with its heavy mail, the tens of thousands of letters to W. J. that streamed into the office made up a deluge of paper. I have seen many offices that bore evidence of heavy work, but never like that. Documents were stacked high on the desk and chairs and on every other available resting place. There were even piles of them on the old horsehair sofa on which W. J. had snatched an occasional nap when he was practicing law. When

Charles asked me to be seated, I chose the chair that had the lowest stack. The amazing thing was that he seemed to know where to put his hand to find anything he wanted, and he was never confused. We hit it off well together from the first. He put all of his cards on the table, or, more accurately, might have done so if there had been a vacant place where he could lay them. Besides the exacting duties in publication he attended to most of W. J.'s correspondence and personal business.

He showed me letters containing invitations to speak and I was surprised at the number. W. J. could scarcely accept all of them in a lifetime and he was to devote less than sixty days to the next Chautauqua season. Some of the letters plaintively stated that the writers had been on the waiting list for years. It was easy to see that here was one lecturer who needed no manager to drum up dates.

I learned of a policy which W. J. had followed for years. With his first bid for presidency he decided that he could not consistently continue in the practice of law for a living because the most lucrative fees stemmed from corporations or from those who had some controversy or business with state or federal government and he barred himself from all such. Anyone would know that he might command whatever price he would name in that kind of practice, and obviously there was nothing either illegal or unprofessional in it, but he charted a course leading to reform in government and he wished no strings, nor substance for suspicion, to be attached to his public work.

Charles Wayland Bryan was forty-two years old at that time. He had been the editor and proprietor of a farm paper, *The American Homestead,* for five years. He had a decided flair for agriculture and was a farmer along with his other activities, for a large share of his life. For one thing he liked to raise mules. Besides, he had been a wholesale dealer in coal and his knowledge of that commodity was valuable when later, as Mayor of Lincoln, he established municipal coalyards when it appeared that the people were not getting a square deal with their fuel. The same conditions, when he was Governor of Nebraska, led him to establish state gasoline filling stations and a state coal company, both of which were operated on a non-profit basis. In 1897 he had become political secretary and business agent for W. J. and continued in that capacity until the Great Commoner died in 1925.

While there was a certain family resemblance in the brothers they did not look at all alike. Charles was tall, erect and rather slender, and wore a mustache. He was quite bald and the direct glare of light was so painful to his eyes that he wore his hat indoors and out, except on more formal occasions when he covered his crown with a black skull cap. In one way the two men were exactly alike, and that was in their inherent honesty. Neither would shun by the breadth of a hair a promise made or implied. But both were so direct and clean-cut in their word that there was little chance for implication. The other most apparent resemblance was in their deep flashing eyes. Brother Charlie's words were rapid and staccato and he used no rounded sentences or figurative phrases.   He was companionable and liked nothing more than congenial friends at the table or a turn at Kelley pool with two or three cronies at the Commercial Club.

I could see that the arrangement of a lecture tour was no easy task and proffered my assistance.   He turned the files over to me and I had found a new job, arduous enough, but most fascinating, and it was one that I enjoyed for years.   He outlined the policy he wished to observe.   The tour should be arranged so that it would demand as little hard travel as possible, but it must be distributed well as to territory.   First consideration should be given to the cities that had been crying for W. J. the longest, and no political consideration should be observed.   I could assign a portion of the available dates to the circuits and he charged me to keep what I wanted for myself.   It required some little of my time for a few weeks to perfect the arrangements, but Charles was pleased with the results.   I am glad I can say that as new managers came into the circuit field, I tried to be unselfish in the allocation of dates even though some of them went to my chief competitors, and the only time Charles ever chided me was when I gave to others some time which he thought I should keep for myself.

A contract for a lecture by Mr. Bryan was like money in the bank.   For the Chautauqua that was fortunate enough to secure it, it was priceless.   The general interest in the session was highly stimulated and the season-ticket sale was enhanced.   In those things he did not participate at all except for the pleasure he felt when others were benefited. No man or association could ever suffer financial loss by engaging him. That he would not agree to at all. If he couldn't draw the money into the box office he would have none of it. First and last, arrangements for thousands of other speakers passed through my hands. Some of them were people of fame and wide repute. I can think of no one of them who would have earned a very modest fee, and many could not have had reimbursement for expenses alone, under a contract like Bryan's. The sponsors of even the headliners must advertise widely and usually sell a large number of season tickets to net enough to pay reasonably high fees. The season tickets were held by the people who represent the cream and bulk of attendance, and in addition to that income, it was rare that any speaker would draw as much as a hundred dollars in single admissions. Bryan's lecture contracts were the same for one city as for all others. I made many of them and have no need for conjecture.

The contract provided some interesting things. For compensation Mr. Bryan would receive the sum of single admissions until two hundred fifty dollars were accounted for. After that his sponsor would receive the same income until his share was also two hundred fifty dollars. All that came from sales in excess of five hundred dollars was divided equally between the two. No sponsor could ask more for a ticket than was charged for at least three other attractions in the course, and in no case could the admission price be more than fifty cents. Printed in the contract was a recommendation that no more than twenty-five cents be charged.

Bryan paid his own expenses and had no part of season-ticket income. For winter lecture courses there was some modification in the arrangements, particularly where reserved seats were involved and seating capacity was limited, but these changes were not important, and anyhow I am dealing with the Chautauqua.

Bryan could deliver a hundred lectures in the space of two months and still have a few days' open time to permit him to speak without pay to religious conventions and Bible Schools, because, unlike most men he could visit two cities, and occasionally three, in one day and deliver a lecture in each.

The puny criticism of the propriety of his Chautauqua lecturing, flowing from poisonous pens and strident voices, never disturbed me any more than it rankled him. The critics must have been misinformed or took no trouble to learn the truth. The lecture platform was practically Mr. Bryan's sole source for income, although there was some from his writing. He and his family lived well but in simple taste, but no one can in truth say that a Bryan was ever niggardly. His expenses for his public work were heavy indeed. His gifts to church, charity, Y. M. C. A. and education drew heavily from his purse. Each year he would decide how much he must earn for all purposes and then assign a sufficient number of weeks in the calendar to be devoted to the platform. When he had made his decision there was little use for anyone to try to effect a change.

Sharp users of unkind words reached to a climactic revelry when Bryan was Secretary of State, and, while

on vacation, made a few Chautauqua speeches for pay.
Other high Government officials could retain private
sources of income in business or profession, and without such I don't see how anyone could serve decently
in the President's cabinet. But when Bryan used a few
days from a vacation period, that is granted to most
men, to engage momentarily in the vocation that provided his livelihood—that was a grave offense. The
simple fact is that he needed some money to pay his
bills and he collected a little of it in his share from that
received from people who paid a quarter or a half dollar to listen to him speak.

I had no share in the arrangements of Mr. Bryan's
early Chautauqua lectures, and have no firsthand
knowledge of the extent of his activities then, or of the
amount of his earnings in that period. Nevertheless,
during my long and—I think—intimate acquaintance
with him, he often alluded to his earlier experiences, and
I believe the results of his efforts were no different from
those that ensued when I had a part in his plans. Substantially his policy at first was quite similar to the
one I knew. From 1909 until he passed from earthly
scenes I had a considerable part in his lecture plans,
and since I made countless engagements for him I am
sure of the truth of what I write.

I have read some very unkind biographies of Bryan
and, during his lifetime, columns of untruthful criticism. In this discussion there is no need for me to concern myself with the sharp complaints of his political
and economic views. If these complaints were based
on the same kind of inaccurate information that is re-

vealed in the words written by his Chautauqua critics, I cannot escape the thought that those people, or any of them who are still alive, should revise their stock of information for the good of their immortal souls.

In my experience, Mr. Bryan's Chautauqua lectures, and substantially all of his lectures on lecture courses, were made on the basis of the agreement of the terms of which I have stated. Occasionally, but very seldom, he might speak for a stipulated fee which, of course, was less than his critics thought. His policy was set in the determination that no one should be out of pocket for engaging him. I knew of some instances when it was found that the committee might suffer a loss. If, for instance, the receipts amounted to three hundred fifty dollars, Bryan's share was two hundred fifty dollars, leaving one hundred dollars for the committee. If he discovered that their expense had amounted to more than one hundred dollars, he would insist upon reimbursing them to the amount of the difference, which made me a little impatient because with a greater effort they might easily have made as much as he could. On the other hand if the meeting were rained out and the receipts were only thirty-five dollars, that was all he would receive, if indeed he took anything at all.

Stories of the amount of his income per lecture were nearly all exaggerated. I have always been surprised and amused with the strange fallacy cherished by people all over America when they estimate the size of an audience. If a thousand people gather on the public square, men like to think there are five thousand. I know of many instances when a crowd in an auditorium was estimated at twenty thousand when I knew there were only ten thousand because I had counted the seats. Those who really know the truth like to permit people to enjoy their little illusions, and somehow the fact of a great concourse of people indicates a kind of grandeur from which people derive pride. In the same way Americans have pleasure in overestimating the population of their cities. Ask the average person how many people live in the town and he will say, "Well, the last census shows a hundred thousand but they missed many people and besides the city has grown a lot since the count was made and we really have about a hundred and thirty thousand people." He is not at all troubled when the next census shows only a hundred and three thousand. This little fallacy, while quite common, is harmless enough. Americans are proud of themselves and their institutions and assembling capacity of their people, and fascinating exaggeration is really only a reflection of their own aspirations. Like many of the other things I know about people that I learned from cattle, I first discovered how to appraise the size of the audience because I had learned how to estimate the number of animals in a herd. Therefore I always could make a pretty good guess of the number of people in an audience, and I could always check my estimates at the box office.

One of the first lectures which Bryan delivered on my circuit was at Blue Rapids, Kansas. Since that was forty-five years ago, I am sure my friends in that lovely little city will not mind my saying the population was then about fifteen hundred people. Of these a thousand, young and old, had season tickets. The tent could not contain even half of the Bryan audience, which did not matter at all because thousands could sit or recline on the grass under the trees, and all hear very well. I think we charged twenty-five cents for admission, and as I remember, the cash receipts were about a thousand dollars. Therefore we had sold four thousand single admission tickets which, with the season ticket holders, if they were all present, made an audience of five thousand people. Naturally the good citizens thought there were as many as ten thousand people on hand, and those who have told such tall tales of Bryan's income might have thought the same if they had been present.

By no means did all of Bryan's lectures yield so much cash, even when we charged fifty cents. The gross receipts were more likely to amount to from three hundred fifty dollars to seven hundred dollars. Sometimes, especially in 1912, when Bryan's spectacular performance at the Baltimore Convention which nominated Woodrow Wilson raised him to a peak in box office popularity, as much as fifteen hundred dollars might be received, but the average was much less. One season he told me that he was going to set aside all the money he might earn in excess of the basic two hundred fifty dollars for each lecture and hoped the total for the whole summer might amount to enough to buy a motorboat. We added up the boat money from time to time, but alas I fear that in the end he had to add to the sum or else content himself with an outboard-motor craft.

On the whole Bryan could make the amount of money he had decided was necessary for the year in a comparatively short period of lecturing, and, as I have said, all of his other speeches were made without pay. On the other hand he might easily have made a fortune. As a somewhat experienced manager, I am sure I could have completed a sufficient number of engagements to net him a quarter of a million dollars in any year and still leave a considerable portion of his time open for other purposes. Such a program would yield a sizable amount, if not as much, for his sponsors, and all of that would have been effected in the terms of a reasonable contract. Had he been exploited as other famous speakers, or stars in other fields, then or now, have been or are exploited, the sum would have been very much larger. He was content to earn merely enough to sustain a splendid if simple home, to provide a decent living for himself and his family, and to accomplish his varied purposes in politics, religion and education.

I do not pretend to know exactly how much income Mr. Bryan received through the years or in any year. Nor do I know how much he gave to people or institutions or to any cause in which he was interested. However, I was intimately acquainted with him and with Charles, and I should say that Mr. Bryan was but moderately well to do until the last few years of his life, and that the larger share of the fortune he left was made from profits in real estate during the last five years that he lived, although none of that has any bearing on his mighty power as a speaker.

With his help I sometimes endeavored to determine the proportion of his paid lectures to the number of speeches he made without fees. I think the former comprised about 20 per cent of the total, and I do not include the countless little talks at luncheons, receptions and wayside stops in his travels. It is evident, therefore, that I can place no credence in the wails of those who charge that Bryan was mercenary or was tempted to resolve into financial gain the great fame which he had achieved.

I frequently accompanied W. J. on his Chautauqua tours, and when that was not possible some one else would go along to ease the burden of travel as much as possible. He was not difficult to manage, no matter how hard was the way. I might show him a memorandum of all details for a week ahead. This would indicate cities he was to visit, the time of arrival and departure, and change in connections for each day. He would read it and so far as I know would not refer to it again, but he never forgot where he was to go, when he must start, or would arrive. Often the travel was difficult. Often it would mean a night train, or maybe two or three. Frequently we must drive with a team and buggy, or in an automobile. At first the latter was not dependable and roads were bad. I could not depend upon one automobile in those days but would provide two or three, so that if one expired we could change to another. When the machines were perfected and roads were improved, our problems were much abated.

He would insist upon paying for all travel expense, and he was very generous in tips for porters, bellboys, waiters and all who served him. Sometimes he would draw a little cash for pocket money, and while I never saw him refer to a memorandum, on settlement days he always knew how much I had advanced. In the beginning I was careful to prepare a carefully checked report of receipts, verified by what I considered to be a competent audit of the figures. He soon stopped that practice. "Just let me know the amount of my share," he would say, and that was the way we followed. In accounting, travel and business transactions he would reduce all operations to the minimum. I have often seen him write a check, drawn on his bank, on a plain slip of paper or even on the half of an envelope slit in two pieces. Nevertheless, Charles told me that W. J. never was mistaken in his knowledge of his balance.

He systematized his mental and physical processes in clear cut and fine economy. He could effect that because of the matchless retentivity of his mind. I have never seen him speak from a manuscript. If there was some sudden and unusual call for a speech—a church dedication, a cornerstone laying or something of the kind—he might prepare a speech for the occasion on an hour's notice. Three or four lines on a slip of paper to indicate the points he would make, and the physical job was done. His facility in words and abundance in memory supplied all the rest.

In the conservation of his mental and physical energy Bryan's skill rests without parallel in my memory. As he moved along no moment in the day was wasted and each was employed purposefully. When I would raid the newsstand and bring him all the papers I could find, he would devour the contents page by page, tear out a column here and an item there, stuff the tatters in his pocket to read again, and shove the rest aside. In a few minutes he had absorbed the news of the day. While his route of travel was not published, there would be telegrams at every stop and a bundle of letters awaited him in each town in which he was scheduled to speak. When he could have a few minutes for himself on a train, he would extract a crushed pad of paper from the ample pocket of his coat, and even if there was no more than a suitcase for a desk he would take a pen or pencil and write many letters and telegrams, or an editorial for *The Commoner*. In any event he would manage to dispose of all of his correspondence, and when it was finished for the time it was completed for good.

Seldom indeed could he enjoy a few minutes of quiet without interruption. Word of his presence would spread through the train and there was an almost constant stream of curious but friendly people up and down the aisle, and most of them must shake hands with him. The greetings from the men who filed past scarcely varied: "Mr. Bryan, I voted for you three times and I just want to shake your hand." I often wondered how he could have failed in the elections since all the people we saw had supported him.

Somehow, probably by rural telephone or word of mouth, news of his journey had been spread about and at every train stop we would hear the shouts of the crowd assembled at the station. Regardless of the import of letter, telegram, or editorial, he would go to the platform to greet his admirers. There was no good for me to protest. He said the people perhaps had made trouble for themselves to come and he would not disappoint them. That was true, I know, because some of them had left their fields or shops and maybe traveled miles to have a fleeting glimpse of the Great Commoner, and possibly grasp his hand for an instant and say they had voted for him three times. Too often the train would begin to move along before all could get within reach.

When we reached a temporary destination there was really acclaim. As the train slowed to a stop we could see flags and banners, and the music of a band would reach our ears. When Mr. Bryan appeared, shouts, steam whistles and automobile horns rent the air. The mayor and committee were on hand and behind them were troops of boy scouts, flocks of flower girls and badge-bedecked school children were herded together by their monitors. Beyond all was the throng of people who crowded the station platform. There is something quite disconcerting and even a bit frightening in the effort of an ordinary person to force a path through a crowd of human beings facing him. Conveying Bryan through a little sea of friendly faces lit by shining eyes was like the passage of the hosts of Israel as they walked between the walls of parted water of the Red Sea. I have thought often of such an experience, repeated for me perhaps hundreds of times. One caught in the grip of a multitude of fellow beings, say in Times Square or Madison Square Garden, or even in a great political campaign, can scarcely escape a sense of the spirit of the mob, and fear the crush in the movement sweeping from the composite mind of an unordered multitude.

I could feel, but even now I cannot describe the difference in the concourse that welcomed Bryan day by day. Surely they did not come because of curiosity. Most of the citizens of our section had seen him before, perhaps often. Many, maybe nearly all, had heard his voice. There was no play of the emotions generated in the heat of a political campaign. No radios were blaring his name or words. The great newspapers of the nation were not presently printing black headlines in praise or fault. True, Bryan was known by more and had been seen by more people than any other human being in the world. Here he came, a simple private citizen engaged in the labor of earning his daily bread.

Even though his welcome by multitudes was ever genuine and kind, I was often puzzled with the quality of it. There was shouting and applause, but neither was tumultuous or vociferant. I could detect no evidence of pent-up feelings or surge of passion such as characterize a political campaign. No lurid advertising had evoked curiosity or sown seeds of unwarranted expectation. But there they were, the unnumbered multitudes from the farms and villages, the cities and railroad yards. I could have wished that they might all have been crowded into the Chautauqua grounds because Mr. Bryan was met by more people without than within. But why were they there, everywhere he went? He was then enacting no crusader's role and bore no promise of political reform. He was merely going from place to place to stand under hot canvas and talk to people about "The Prince of Peace," or "The Value of an Ideal."

Later, at exactly the appointed moment, we would escort him quietly into the tent from the rear so that only a few people could see him enter. All the hard seats were filled, and around the edge of the open canvas cover people would stand, ten, twenty or thirty persons deep. When Mr. Bryan was introduced the audience would clap their hands, some of them would shout, and down in Texas there would issue a wave of rebel yells. Once again, I was puzzled with the subdued gentleness even in the warmest applause. I have been in embassy gatherings and meetings in affairs of state and have been told that the modest hand clapping was an evidence of the good taste of those present. No doubt that is true, but if that was an expression of taste and breeding, so was this. Or was this something that came from a deeper recess in human hearts? Bryan would stand with a smile on his face, with a fan in his hand, doing nothing, acting nothing, to prolong the expression of welcome. In a moment or two he would raise his arm, the palm of his hand turned to the people and a quiet would come like the fall of a rose leaf on the grass.

In July, 1925, I rode, as an honorary pallbearer, in the sad cortege that followed W. J. Bryan's catafalque from the New York Avenue Presbyterian Church in Washington to Arlington Cemetery. With me were two former members of President Wilson's Cabinet, a well-known United States Senator, a Congressman and another former official in the Wilson administration. They were talking, of course, of our departed friend. One spoke of that gesture, hand raised high with the palm turned towards the people. A gesture that had brought an expectant calm to a multitude a thousand times and more. It was, they agreed, nothing less than majestic. I had seen that raised arm, ah, hundreds of times. It was, at once, a command and a benediction, and it seemed to transmit a feeling of peace.

Again and again I placed myself so that I could look into the faces of the people as he spoke. I could sense and see the evidence of their emotions but no sound from it would reach my ears. For an hour and a half I thought they were enjoying a deep feeling of peace and even happiness. Most of them, I suppose, usually carried in their hearts the same kind of worries and fears that perplex men in all places and stations. Here, for a little while, these would slip away from their consciousness and they could reach towards the stars.

Was all of this caused by the stirring power of great oratory? Not exactly. Those people were silent, except that now and then a wave of applause would sweep across the tent, or a smile would expand into a ripple of laughter, but both would fall into silence as abruptly as the sound of them had burst. They were almost motionless, too. I saw no nudging of elbows nor a glance aside into a neighbor's eyes, or even a shift of weight from one tired foot to another among those who stood. Certainly they did not appear to be chained to the spot, but all of them, with strong bodies or weak ones, clothed in good raiment or covered by the garments of labor and the farm, seemed almost literally to float on a placid plane. I think what I am trying to say is that physical sensations seemed to be suspended for a time. Perhaps the poise and calm of the speaker had something to do with it. Whatever motion there was in him was like the rhythm of a mountain stream flowing through the rocks. He scarcely moved on his feet. One hand held a palm leaf fan which was never still. The other rested alternately on a block of ice in a basin on the table, and then on top of his head upon which the heat beat down pitilessly. Even his frequent gestures seemed to be extensions of those motions. Water would stream down his face for he had the hottest place in an acre of discomfort, but he, too, seemed unaware of fatigue or heat.

I do not know to what extent those people had enshrined Bryan as an ideal in their thoughts, if at all. I have tried to discover for myself the reason or reasons for the phenomenon I witnessed so many times, and I think I found three. They may be only theories but they are the only explanations I can find to add to the undoubted perfection of the greatest orator I have ever heard. First, those people may have sensed in Bryan a greatness of spirit that perhaps escaped those who were never present on a like occasion. Second, they heard the voice of a man they esteemed expressing in clear words the best fruit of their own meditations and the very peak of their aspirations even though these were usually hidden within themselves. Finally, if we can accept at all the proposition that the affection which one man bears for another is reciprocated by the latter, that proposition may furnish part of the explanation. Bryan loved people and had a faith in them that was sublime. He believed that if they could and would act and think according to their best instincts, that altogether they possessed a power that could move and save the world. Perhaps, after all, the enraptured state of mind of the Chautauqua audience reflected the stirring of power within its composite heart. Perhaps a similar awakening may explain why a mighty unity of the force of hand and will could win a global war in 1945. I think there is but one word that can correctly define the feeling of the Chautauqua audience for Mr. Bryan. There was respect, of course, admiration and even affection. But over all there was one quality which seemed never to be absent, and that was reverence.

I do not see how anyone who did not hear Bryan speak could have a concept of the force of his words. One biographer who was sometimes at fault in his facts, and more often unfair in his analysis, wrote an apt distinction between his spoken and written words. He said the words of a speech were orchestrated for his own remarkable voice. The quality of the sound that flowed from his lips enhanced the value of the words. He would emphasize by letting his voice fall a little as though there was a period following the accented word, or he would effect the same result by raising the tone. His sentences were clear-cut and never confused in arrangement. They were accurately keyed and there was little or no transposition from the key when he reached a climax. The tonal quality of his voice surpassed that of any other speaker or speakers I have ever heard. Every syllable was uttered so distinctly that no one need cup a hand behind his ear to hear its full import. He had read some in Latin and Greek and in poetry and philosophy, and with his retentive mind had garnered a very extensive vocabulary. Nevertheless it was noteworthy that he chose the words that most people could understand without effort. If his audience numbered a thousand people or ten thousand, there could be no one in it who could not hear distinctly. Once or twice, on a quiet summer evening I have stood at a distance of a block away and even then I could hear what he said. His tones would never swell to a shout nor break into a roar. When the volume expanded in a climactic phrase, there was no loss in the fullness and music of the tone. Along with the melody of his voice and grace of his gestures, the flash of his eyes would seem to reach even to those who sat far away.

There was method in all of this as there was design in what he said. He told me that he always tried to speak in a way that would require of the people the least possible mental and physical exertion to understand what he said and thus they could use their minds without interference to understand what he meant. That is the reason he did not perplex them with unfamiliar words. Many would say that his voice would "carry" farther than that of anyone else. That was foolish, he thought. In a given volume of sound one voice would carry as far as any other. The reason he could be heard at a great distance was because he enunciated every syllable clearly and distinctly and would not permit the sound of one word to crowd into the tone of another.

As I offer this characterization of Bryan's Chautauqua speeches I would not say at all that it could apply to his political speeches. Indeed, Chautauqua lectures and political speeches are so entirely different it would be difficult to make comparisons. In a political campaign applause, for instance, is as likely to be malevolent as it is commendatory.

I was well inured to travel but when I kept up with Bryan for a couple of weeks I was exhausted, and I didn't need to make the speeches. On some particularly difficult days he was tired, but with a few hours, and sometimes a few moments of sleep, traces of fatigue would disappear. He would drop into slumber in a moment, in a train coach, or with his head resting on the back of a seat in an automobile. When he finished an address thousands of people would press forward to shake hands. He would sit on the edge of the platform and grasp the hands of all comers, using his left hand as well as his right. When he had been surrounded by throngs at the stations or in the hotels, and I would suggest that we should find, somehow, a few minutes for relaxation, and delay his appearance a bit, he would say that he could relax better when he was speaking. He is the only person I ever knew who could rest physically while he was making a speech and that was because his mental and body functions were so well coordinated.

Much has been written about his capacity for food, and most of it was of the same kind of legend as other inaccurate stories of him. My managerial associations began while he was still under fifty years of age. He was large and strong and had the appetite of a healthy man. His physical endurance surpassed that of most other men and, measured by a requirement of the body of a hard worker, he needed plenty of food and enjoyed it too. No kind of viands would disagree with him, and I often wished I had as good a digestion as he had. The tales of his ravenous eating were terribly exaggerated. On occasion, he made a score or more of speeches in a day—the majority of them unscheduled. That requires much fuel in food. I have seen many hearty men who ate more than he did. Stories of the unseeming quantity of food he consumed were nearly as untruthful as a statement that he got drunk on alcohol, which he never tasted.

The tale of his fondness for grape juice was as amusing and fallacious as any. As a matter of fact, he did not care for the beverage at all, although there were many times when he had to sip the refreshing drink, because people were always bringing it around, just as they were wont to flood Vice-President Fairbanks with buttermilk, which he didn't care much about. Sometimes a manufacturer would send a case of some new fruit drink to Bryan and when it reached us en route, it had to be distributed among those who cared for it and then the legend would grow some more. When Mr. Bryan was Secretary of State, and more for decorative purposes than for any other reason, Mrs. Bryan served grape juice, the story of the Commoner's fondness for the drink got out of bounds. One time a brewer sent us a case of what came to be called "near beer," and asked for Bryan's opinion of it. Mr. Bryan replied that he had never tasted beer, and was incompetent to judge, but he complimented the man for turning his attention to non-alcoholic beverages.

I have written in space of Mr. Bryan because I think he was the greatest speaker in the Chautauqua, and because I think he did more to enliven and extend the movement than anyone else. His passing from the platform marked the beginning but not the cause of the decline of the force radiating from the tents. I wanted very much to write a biography of him, while my rich experience was new in my mind. I had planned to begin the effort after the close of the 1925 season. My last letter from him was written from Dayton, Tennessee, a few days before his death. He spoke of the project and told me he could give me some time for the purpose that autumn. He also reproached me a little because I had not arranged to spend part of my time in Florida, which he loved so much. He had always urged me to buy a lot and build a little home there so that I could be near him at least for a few months in the year. In that letter he told me that if I would accept it, he would buy a lot for me. I went to Miami in September and bought the lot, but alas, I had followed in the sad procession which left his mortal remains in Arlington in July.

AS THEY ROLLED ALONG

I hope I have given no impression that Chautauqua people were glum, sober, vain and sanctimonious. The opposite of such adjectives could better describe them. By the time the talent had swept past the first nine towns on the circuit, and thus had come to know all the crews, platform managers and junior girls, everybody was acquainted and a guild of happy friendships had been established. The talent regarded their work seriously enough but had a great deal of fun in doing it. A few of the townspeople could always be included in the friendly circle. The junior girls and the crews could be depended upon to plan a party after the show. When platform togs had been changed and the tent was lashed for the night, the folks would be found back of the platform ready for a short hour of fun. They ate melons and ice cream, or perhaps from a huge box of fried chicken donated by one of the good women of the town. These little gatherings were much like the jam sessions of latter-day dance bands. The performers performed little new original stunts and indulged in many quips at each other, and, I suppose, even more at the expense of the managers. The girls would collect the soiled linen of the performers and have it fresh and clean at a later stand.

The tastes of individual lecturers were always remembered, and so there was a tub filled with ice and watermelons ready when Opie Read came to town. The parties did not last long because lights had to be out at a certain hour. Sometimes the performers must repair to the depot and perhaps wait a long time for a late train. When finally automobiles were adopted for transportation of everybody, often enough the talent might drive well into the night to shorten the time of travel next day.

On their part, the managers had their moments of sport when they discussed the talent. One lecturer may have been spoken of as an encyclopedia man, not because he was particularly erudite, but because he had fashioned his oratorical offering from books rather than from life. Little beginning concert companies were called tingalings, and the most brilliant of all the talent were good merchandise.

There was a fine bond of friendship existing among the people of all the component parts, and no thought of class. Even the actors from Broadway, after a few days of bewilderment, fitted into the happy combination, and we learned again that people from one section or station were about the same as those of all the others. There was never any reference to rubes or hicks or yokels or the sticks, perhaps because most of us were pretty close to rural scenes and habits.

I rarely saw even the mightiest orator reprove his listeners. In fact I remember of but one instance, and that was humorous enough to fall short of offense. On a hot afternoon the audience of a certain worthwhile speaker was sweltering in the tent. Nearly every one on the benches was wielding a fan because there were always local advertisers who took care that fans were in every seat. The flutter of fans disturbed the speaker to the point of exasperation. Finally he paused and glared at the poor people. "I know it is hot," he said, "I'm hot, too. If you must fan please fan in unison, like this." And he moved his hands back and forth. "Now, altogether, right, left, right, left." And so he drilled them, then he went on with his address which was so interesting that people soon forgot to fan.

The courtesy extended to the speaker by the audience was usually reciprocated in kind. Very early we found that little children, most welcome for the entertainment part of the program, were restless and mischievous when the lecturer appeared. The junior girl soon had the youngsters in hand and she would march them off to a shady spot for an hour of storytelling. But babies were something else. The wail of an infant is hard on a speaker. Yet that old quip about "crying babies being like good resolutions and should be carried out" was rarely spoken. One speaker became pretty nervous when the mother of a poor little crying child cuddled and rocked the infant in her arms. Finally he said, "Madam, I give it as my considered opinion that what that baby needs is not lodging but food."

One afternoon the great Senator Dolliver was addressing a Chautauqua audience at Pawnee City, Nebraska. As his matchless eloquence thundered from the platform, a baby began to scream. The poor mother made haste to leave when the Senator stopped her. "Don't go, madam. The natural function of an infant is to cry. Anyone who doesn't know that hasn't sense enough to understand my speech. I like babies and they don't bother me at all. They don't bother other mothers in the tent, and as for you frowning sons-of-guns of men, it's none of your confounded business what the baby does."

Speaking of babies, I think the following incident is unusual. The Chautauqua was going well in Pawhuska, Oklahoma. That was a long time ago. There were many blanket Indians in the vicinity and a good share of the population in the city had some Indian blood. Those Indians were handsome people and seemed to enjoy the Chautauqua very much. I visited the tent one hot afternoon. Quite in front and on one side were seated some twenty or so bucks, wearing their blankets over bare torsos. On the opposite side was a similar group of Indian women, and they, too, wore Indian garb. Many of them were wealthy, or at least had money as oil had begun to flow down there. At the rear end of the tent I found a row of Indian babies. The beautiful little creatures were decked out in colorful raiment. Though flies pestered their sticky little faces and hands, there was no whimper from any of them. Each infant was fastened to the board upon which the mother carries her child on her back, and each board was laid across a very expensive baby cab.

One hot summer evening Judge George D. Alden of Boston was addressing his audience in an Iowa town. Alden, a lineal descendant of John and Priscilla, was a most charming and effective speaker. As usual, he was garbed in evening dress and his rhetoric was choice. The tent was pitched at the edge of a cow pasture from which, it was supposed, the cattle had been removed. One lonely animal, however, had, somehow returned to her habitat. She bellowed a lonely moo from some distance away and no one paid much attention to it. Evidently she decided to investigate the big tent with its bright lights. She came closer and closer, mooing all the way. Finally she stuck her head under the very edge of the tent and uttered a particularly loud and mournful cry. The audience was convulsed. Adrian Newens who shared platform time with the judge was in a front seat enjoying himself hugely. The grin on Adrian's face was more exasperating to the speaker than the interruption by bossie, and he yelled, "Adrian Newens, can't you do something to stop that cow?" Newens rose and said, "Judge Alden, that lecture we are forced to listen to lacks some of the dramatic elements of the interpolations of yonder bovine. I suggest that you accept her valuable assistance and proceed with your speech."

Those Chautauqua speakers were quick in retort and clever in turning an unfortunate incident to their own advantage. Everyone knew that W. J. Bryan was a devout exponent of prohibition and a bitter enemy of strong drink. One evening his daughter, Ruth Bryan, graced the platform in Fort Collins, Colorado. There was a drizzle of rain outside and a pool of water collected in a sag in the tent, almost over the speaker's head. The foreman of the crew knew that he should interrupt the proceedings and take a pole and push the tent upwards so the water could drain off the roof. He waited, hoping that the canvas would hold, but his hope was in vain. The cloth broke and a bucketful of water splashed to the floor. Ruth Bryan smiled at her audience and said, "My friends, you are present on an historic occasion. This is the first time a Bryan ever spoke on a wet platform."

Strickland Gilliland, of dry but hilarious humor, was like that. He is the Hoosier poet who has enriched the language. Nearly every person in the country knows his famous railroad rhyme of "Off agin, on agin, gone agin, Finnegan." He wrote a poem on fleas which he said was the shortest in the world. It was, "Adam had 'em." Gilliland would not appear until after the platform manager had finished the introduction. Then he would stroll on, with a stick or the stem of a weed he had picked up, and he broke the thing into bits while he solemnly looked his audience over. One time after he had begun his speech he called to a waiting crewman in the wings, for some water. It was almost as unusual for a Chautauqua speaker to sip water when he was performing as it was for him to use notes. The boy was perplexed. He wondered if Gilliland had some demonstration in mind and whether he wanted a pail or a pan or a glass of the liquid. So he said, "Do you want it to drink?" "No, lad," was the answer, "I always make a high dive in the last act."

On one occasion Strick was introduced by a local celebrity. Usually introductions must be said in a dozen words or so. This time the introducer made the most of his opportunity to exhibit his oratorical talent. He went on and on while the people became restless and squirmed in their seats. Meanwhile Gilliland was waiting in the wings. When the talkative but kind man had finished with his eloquence, Gilliland stuck his head through the curtains, held up a hand, and said, "Just a minute, folks, before you go."

J. Adam Bede, for years Congressman from Minnesota, had a sense of humor that was sublime. It was as spontaneous as it was real. He was well named "The Humorist of the House." I think he more nearly resembled Bill Nye than any other speaker I have in mind. He was good for a return trip over any circuit as often as he could be secured. One day he went into Harry Harrison's office in Chicago. Harry, a six-footer and a fine executive, is boyish in his enthusiasm and idealism, and as ingenuous as a child. He likes to express his code in a very few words. On this occasion he had a card fastened to the wall. The words on it were, "When in doubt tell the truth." Bede read it quizzically and said, "That's a good idea, Harry, but the trouble with you is that you are never in doubt."

Young people today, and even old ones who did not travel a great deal forty years ago, can have no concept of the difficulties attending the necessity of a group of people reaching a certain point each day, regardless of transportation and weather conditions. If the trains did not run, or if a trip was too long to make by horses, the difficulties were increased. The trains on branch lines, as a rule did not run on Sunday. One Sunday we had planned to convey our talent from Grand Island to Ord, Nebraska, by automobile. That was all right in dry weather, but it was not dry in Grand Island.

Rain fell in torrents. It was in 1910, and the road was but little more than a trail. An automobile could not get through at all. I happened to be in Grand Island, a division point of the Union Pacific Railroad, and I managed to secure a special train. There were only about six people to carry but we had a full complement of equipment. Those six people climbed into a long coach and spread their baggage over as many seats as possible and then unpacked some of their clothes, that were wet from previous rains, and hung them all over the car. It was pretty expensive but they made the date, the first, last and prime objective of all the talent.

One day in that same year I had Mr. Bryan scheduled to speak in Garnett, Kansas, in the afternoon, and at Paola in the evening. There was no train available. The manager at Garnett secured what he said was the finest auto in the country to carry us. He also had a skilled mechanic to accompany the driver and I had to pay sixty dollars for the trip. After Paola it was necessary to drive on to Kansas City in time to take a train at eleven thirty for Iowa. Because of the fame of mechanic and car, I did not take the usual precaution of securing an extra vehicle. We got to Paola although the fine auto balked some along the way. We spoke Bryan early, at six thirty, to allow plenty of time to reach Kansas City. Now Paola is perhaps forty miles from Kansas City, and on the fine highway today most motorists would scorn to make the trip in more than three-quarters of an hour. It wasn't like that that evening in 1910. We must have traveled a much greater distance and were frequently lost as the gas lights on the car expired soon after dark. The men tried hard enough. The mechanic had the floor boards of the car removed and was tinkering with some of the machinery all the time. The thing would run a while and then stop. After more coaxing it would snort along for a time, but always stopped again. Once, one of the men aroused some people in a darkened farmhouse and came back with a bar of soap from which he cut shavings and fed them into the machine. We were four hours and a half on the way and missed the train.

That, I can say in truth, was one of the very few occasions in my whole Chautauqua experience when we failed to "make the date," but the difficulties we encountered were in the common experience of all the travelers.

With a journey ended for a day, the talent could not always be at ease. In many places hotels were none too good, and even at that many of them had no dining room. Often refuge was found in the home of some kindhearted citizen and the crew boys had always spotted the best place for food.

Alton Packard, one of the brightest of star entertainers, classified hotels in little towns as one-towel, two-towel and three-towel establishments. In the latter the waitress would come to the guest and announce, "Beefsteak, pork chops or cold meats." In the second she would say, "Beefsteak or ham and eggs." In the third she asked only, "How do you want your eggs."

By present-day standards transportation facilities weren't good. Judge Estelle, a Chautauqua lecturer, needed to change from one railroad to another at Wichita, Kansas. He dismounted from his train, gave his baggage to a driver of a horse-drawn hack, and said, "Take me to the other depot." The driver whipped up his team, made a turn in the street and stopped at the curb just across the street. The Judge had had a ride of about seventy-five feet. The driver unloaded the baggage, grinned, and said, "That will be two bits, Cap. I hated to do it but I sure need the money." Estelle was game. He handed the chap a dollar and said, "Keep the change."

Many villages were quite arbitrary and positive in their idea of a proper speed for automobiles. It was not unusual to see signs "Speed limit ten miles per hour" or even eight and sometimes twelve. A Chautauqua man had an experience in such a place. He missed his train connection one night and had a very long jump to be made somehow. He hired a car and driver and set out. Early in the morning the two came to a village with a speed sign. The lecturer, having been up all night, had asked the driver to slow down a bit so he could have a little nap. The driver said he was not exceeding the twelve miles per hour that was lawful in the village through which they were passing. A man on a bicycle, who had been hiding at the side of the road, whistled the travelers to a stop, exhibited a badge of a town marshal and took the autoist off for trial. The office of the judge was in a barber shop. The marshal told his prisoners not to go away, and left the building. In a little while he returned with the Justice of the Peace, who explained that it took him a while to "git" there because he was plowing corn and was at " 'tother end." Then he lapsed into silence. No one said anything. Finally the lecturer, thinking of the miles yet to be traveled, took matters into his own hands. He asked what he was charged with. The marshal said fast driving.

"How fast," asked the prisoner, "do you say we were riding?" "I don't know," was the verdict of the officer, "but I measured things and you were goin' better'n twelve miles."

Again there was silence finally broken by the lecturer. "Well, what are you going to do about it?" The Justice came to life. "They most generally pay thirteen dollars," he said.

"That's a pretty high price, isn't it?"

"Wall, that's what they generally pay."

"Do you mean then," said the prisoner, "that you want me to pay you thirteen dollars?"

"That's what they been apayin'."

There was nothing to do but produce the money as the lecturer thought of the journey ahead. He asked for a receipt. The Justice said his hands were pretty stiff and told the culprit to write out a receipt for him to sign. That was when the lecturer got a little satisfaction. He composed a receipt which the law officer signed without reading as he said he didn't have his specs with him. Following, as I remember, is what was written:

Received the sum of thirteen bucks
From a tourist bold, by heck,
Who traveled fast through our town
And durned near broke his neck.
Now let that be a lesson
When again this way you come,
For ridin' fast through our town
Comes pretty high, by gum.

After all, who would not wish to find again a peaceful
little village where the accompaniment of daily action
is not in constant allegro.

One evening just at the opening of the Chautauqua
in Wellington, Kansas, a terrific storm struck that
charming city. It was during that same series of
floods to which I have alluded elsewhere. Inches of
rain fell and continued well into the night. What
was ordinarily the bed of a dry stream became a
raging torrent. Much property and the lives of people
were in danger. The foreman of the crew, a fine
handsome lad, was Donald Plumb. He had been
doubling in ticket sales. He was quite a hero during
the big storm. He plunged into the raging waters
again and again and assisted helpless people to escape.
When I saw him afterwards he was trying to find his
way into the pockets of his trousers which had been
soaked for hours. He was carrying a considerable share
of the season ticket receipts in checks and cash. One
can imagine the state of the checks. All were stuck
together and the words of many were impossible to
decipher.

He tried to be good humored about it, just as was a very efficient foreman of a crew in Northwestern Nebraska, whose care and setting of his tent was ever a model. A wind storm struck his carefully stretched big top and tore it loose and finally lifted and carried it away. As the canvas broke loose from its guy stakes, the foreman dashed after it with a shipping tag on which he had written RETURN TO REDPATH-HORNER CHAUTAUQUAS, KANSAS CITY, Mo., and tied the bit of paper to a rope of the vanishing tent.

There was one Chautauqua group which appeared to be somewhat mysterious in identity and purpose although its members had no reason or desire to hide their identity. Yet many people wondered what and who were the DC's. The question is asked occasionally even now. Ten managers, several of them in sharp competition in operation, often gathered for mutual counsel. The ten were Crawford Peffer, Keith Vawter, Harry and Vernon Harrison, Arthur Coit, Louis Alber, Paul Pearson, J. R. Ellison, C. H. White and this author. They met two or three times a year, usually at Atlantic City. The time of such meetings was spent in some horseplay, but also in much discussion designed to be of mutual interest and help. Some of the men smoked, and Paul Pearson would produce a box of his favorite brand of cigars which happened to be Chancellor. The men got to calling themselves the Chancellors. They exchanged bulletins often and usually headed them, instead of "Dear Chancellors," merely DC's. So there is a simple answer to what was once a mystery.

SPELL THEM IN CAPS

Any writer who may propose to make a list of all of the Chautauqua speakers, must set himself to a job of research far greater than I am able to undertake. If he wishes to make a comparative analysis of their merits, measured by any standard he may select, he had better secure a large staff for a long quest. I would think that a proper standard would be a sort of yardstick that would measure three things: the drawing power of the speaker, the content of his address, and the degree of permanence in the impression made. Many would rate high in the last two qualities, and could fail in the first. After an experience of twenty-five years as a lecturer manager, I cannot testify that, as a class, the men who were rated as headliners contributed more to the education and enjoyment of the people than the larger number of speakers whose names were not printed in capital letters. The offerings of the latter endowed richly the substance of the movement and many of them became quite famous within that field, although their names were not widely known outside. As to them, my feelings are the same as towards the crew boys. But there were so many of them, that, regardless of their fine contribution to a truly great American movement, the mere listing of their names would require much space, and an appraisal of their worth would stretch, perhaps, into volumes.

I cannot, either, write a complete list of those whom managers liked to advertise as headliners, nor can I define the word, except to say that they were, roughly, those who were supposed to possess ability as public speakers, and had achieved a more or less national reputation in their own fields, chiefly in government and politics. Certainly in many cases a manager would have a hard time to prove they were top notchers, if he accepted his box office figures as the only test. Those whom I name or discuss are really selected rather to convey an idea of the trend and type of public opinion than for any other purpose, and I confine myself to the ones I had sufficient opportunity to observe.

It is often said, with much truth, that the Chautauqua was an important factor in the awakening and development of the so-called Progressive political movement in the first dozen years of this century. Besides those speakers I have named elsewhere, others, such as Ida Tarbell, Lincoln Steffens and Dr. Harvey W. Wiley, challenged the attention of forward-looking people who flocked to their platforms. I believe that is true, but it is scarcely accurate to say it was so planned. Managers were astute enough to seek speakers who were forthright and could talk about the things the people were thinking about. Men of that type were quite aggressive in advancing their views and were quickly attracted to the platform where they could find a thoughtful audience that would listen and not interrupt. If the Chautauqua nurtured Progressive thought it used no partisan cradle. I hope I may be

accepted as truthful when I say partisan politics were
not discussed on the platform and speakers carried no
political or church label.   It is quite true that many of
my good Republican friends charged me with providing
too many Democratic speakers, especially after I had
served as chief of a national speaker's bureau in a
couple of presidential campaigns.   The records do not
prove the charge, nor can that kind of blame be attached to any other manager I knew.

I have selected the names of thirty-three men in the
political field, men whom I respected highly and who
were broad-minded and constructive speakers in the
Chautauqua.

I have chosen nine governors of states.   Hadley and
Folk of Missouri, Hoch of Kansas, Sheldon of Nebraska, Pinchot of Pennsylvania, Patterson of Tennessee, Charles W. Bryan of Nebraska, Brough of
Arkansas, and Glenn of North Carolina.   Of the nine,
four were Republicans and five were Democrats.

While we presented many members of the House of
Representatives, nine of them stand out most clearly
in my mind.   They were George of New York, Bede
of Minnesota, Murdock of Kansas, Rainey of Illinois
(later speaker of the house), McKinley of California,
Scott of Kansas, Champ Clark (who became a truly
great Speaker of the House), Aswell of Louisiana, and
Hobson of Alabama.   Of the nine, there were five
Democrats and four Republicans.   Likewise ten men
who were (or in one case had been) United States
Senators, will live longest in my memory, of those in
that group.   They were LaFollette of Wisconsin, Taylor

of Tennessee, Dolliver and Cummings of Iowa, Norris Brown of Nebraska, Gore of Oklahoma, Cannon of Utah, Pat Harrison of Mississippi, Allen of Kansas, and the sainted Norris of Nebraska. Four of the ten were Democrats and six were Republicans.

Then I take five more who need not be thought of as officeholders, but were prominent in politics. The five were Francis J. Heney, Warren G. Harding, Judge Ben Lindsey, William Howard Taft, and W. J. Bryan. Mr. Taft's Chautauqua tour was short indeed. The Kansas heat was intense, and an illness overtook him so that he was compelled to cancel many of his engagements. Of the five there were three Democrats and two Republicans. So it will be seen that in the thirty-three, we had seventeen Democrats and sixteen Republicans, and I don't see how political affiliations could be divided with a finer line, although no attempt was made to apportion them in that manner, but that was the way it happened.

On the whole I think that of those mentioned above, with the exception of W. J. Bryan, the Republicans among them contributed more to the progressive political thought than the Democrats, and some of them lived long enough to ally themselves to what we now call the New Deal. The Republicans found themselves spoken of either as Standpatters or Progressives, or maybe Bull Moosers.

Very few men in public life served longer than Senator Norris of Nebraska, and certainly none enjoyed more fully the genuine respect and affection of the American people. He spent the summer of 1910 on the Premier Circuit, and that was on the eve of his successful fight against "Cannonism" in the House of Representatives. The drums were never beaten loudly for him and he was neither an emotional nor a dramatic speaker. His manner was quiet and he spoke in a conversational tone, but he made friendships along the way that seemed to ripen into affection with the years.

Gifford Pinchot came along in 1913. He was very much in the public eye as a stalwart friend of Theodore Roosevelt. In my opinion he was the best-informed man in, and the strongest advocate of, the conservation of our natural resources of that period. He was a thoroughly affable, gentlemanly figure on the platform, and his traveling companions responded to his personality almost with the vim of a rooting section at a college football game.

He was one of the only two men, of all the speakers, with whom I had an argument that moved into some very sharp words. We had signed a contract together some months before and shortly before the beginning of the season he wrote me that he wished to cancel it. I fear my reply, which he resented, was altogether too harsh and provocative, and we had it out the first time I met him at the railroad station in McPherson, Kansas. That was one of the letters I have always wished I had written differently. He filled all of his dates without further complaint, and when I mentioned the matter of our little controversy in my office in Washington twenty years later, he seemed to have forgotten the incident. I held him in high esteem, an esteem which I shared for Mrs. Pinchot, with whom I was associated in a National War Relief campaign in Washington in 1942. If the people of the Middle-west did not derive great value from his lectures they were shortsighted, for there are few places where the gospel of soil conservation is needed more.

As I try to retrace the road of things that made up the golden memory of the days of the early Circuits, and endeavor to fit again the personalities of certain great men into their ancient places of my most vivid recol-lections, I must ascribe one of the highest spots to Champ Clark. The great Missouri Congressman gave me a portion of his time during three seasons and was of my first headliners. He was exceedingly scrupu-lous in his observance of details in appearance and words. In 1907, after business arrangements had been completed, he wrote me inquiring carefully the hour of each appearance so that he could provide proper apparel for either afternoon or evening. He had a like fidelity in the preparation of his address. It would be written carefully and then committed to memory. There was a chastity in his words as well as a poetic glow. His humor had a quaint quality but there was nothing whimsical in his speech. I should say that as a speaker he displayed as fine an example of good taste as I have ever seen. In appearance he was a heroic figure that evoked visions of the dignity and grace of ancient statesmen. I heard him speak at a dinner celebrating W. J. Bryan's birthday, in 1911. There were many visiting statesmen and many speeches, but for sheer beauty and glowing color in words, the address of Clark was one of the finest I ever had heard.

It was with Mr. Clark that I had my other little quarrel. That was early in 1908, and southern Kansas was being punished with fearsome floods. Roads and rail tracks were washed away. Travel was uncertain and even hazardous, and mail was delayed. All of our connections were in confusion. Several speakers were stranded in one town and there was a void in another. I came to one of the former and was told that Clark was looking for me and appeared to be disturbed. I searched for him at once and must confess that I was in a bad state of mind and sorely perplexed. Needed remittances had not arrived and I was put to it to keep things moving at all. Warren G. Harding, always genial and calm, joined me as I looked for Mr. Clark. When I found him I was in a temper, quite unjustified because the Congressman was surely not responsible for my woes.

The simple fact is that no checks at all had reached him and he was very properly disturbed. He lost no time when we met, in complaining to me about it. He had been informed that he should collect a certain amount in each of the few preceding towns, and delayed mails had not brought the funds to the men in charge, so they could not pay. I afterwards knew well enough that the chief cause for his complaint arose from the fine care he always employed in keeping his part of a bargain. I am ashamed of the temper I displayed. I told him not to worry about it, that I would have all the money ready for him and that in the future, if he desired, I would see that his fee was counted into his hand on the platform before he need begin his speech. That was an insipience, but Warren Harding laughed a lot about it and always rallied me whenever I saw him in the future. I am glad that Clark forgave me. I went to see him soon after he had been elected to the speakership of the House. The waiting room was filled with people and one or two of them told me they had been waiting for days to see him. Mr. Clark saw me from his private office, and beckoned me in. His room was filled with books and he began to talk about all sorts of things, chiefly, I think, about poetry. He had just been reading some of Walt Mason's rhymes and was in a genial mood. I was nervous because I could not forget all the people outside. When I rose to go, he made me sit down and continued to talk. Finally I said, "Really, Mr. Speaker, I am embarrassed to take so much of your time when so many others are waiting." "Sit down," he said, "I want to talk to you. It does me so much good to see a man who doesn't want a government job that I want you to stay as long as you can." So I remained until he looked at the clock and observed that it was time for the House to convene, and I went along my way very happy that he was too fine to recall the impertinence of a young manager, still in his twenties. In any event, after our flooded-city episode we sometimes made a little ritual of the pay ceremonies. I would hand him his check with a show of formality, and on one occasion he in turn passed it on to a splendid young stripling whom he introduced as his son, Bennet Clark, who later became the very able senior Senator from Missouri.

The case of W. J. Bryan and Champ Clark when, at the Baltimore Convention, the former threw his mighty influence to Woodrow Wilson, thus effecting his nomination, was by no means the only instance in which my affections were in paradoxical confusion. Mr. Bryan mentioned the matter often to me. I am sure he had a great liking for the Missourian who but for Bryan would have been nominated, and he regretted the necessity which compelled the action. To Speaker Clark, the war became a solemn and grim affair. He gave solid and emphatic support to the war effort. In one conversation I had with him in 1918, I learned again of his centered affection on the young officer, his son, who made a good record for himself in the conflict. Champ Clark's love for his family and his neighbors at Bowling Green, Missouri, was, I think, symbolic of his patriotism. Had political fortune not deserted him at Baltimore, I am one who believes the nation would still have been well served.

Both Conservative and Progressive political thinking were in flux during the first dozen years of this century, to as great a degree as in any other period in American history. One who was in touch with the spokesmen for either could sense and almost see the surge of forces moving the public mind. These forces were at work in the minds of the speakers themselves. Senator Jonathan Dolliver, of Iowa, surely of a positive and forceful type and a true Republican, thundered a ringing challenge to forward-looking and independent citizens.

Perhaps no one did more to crush old political structure barriers to a new freedom of thought than Senator Robert M. LaFollette the elder. He was the only speaker I knew who could unwind the mazy, dusty warp of tariff and knit it into an understandable and lovely pattern. By his magical touch even Schedule "K" of the Taft Tariff Bill was spread in vivid array, and vested itself in the clarity and drama of a scene from Shakespeare. He was the most dramatic, and I should add, the most nearly vocally unrestrained, of all the headliners. To permit decent space of time for musical preludes and other program features, the usual Chautauqua lecture was limited to an hour in length. Headliners might go on for an hour and a half, but the brilliant Wisconsin Senator might speak for three hours or even longer.

A scene in Seward, Nebraska, on a hot Sunday afternoon is etched deeply in my memory. The lovely little park on the Blue River was alive with people, and unending circles of wagons and buggies, their horses fighting flies, ringed the enclosure. Even the slanting rays of the sinking sun found the people panting under the sweltering canvas, or reclining under the more welcome shade of trees outside. The fiery little Senator held their attention during the long afternoon. His pompadour would bristle with each fresh attack, and his hands and arms flash in their orbit with the grace of an oriole. The engines of a couple of special trains idled away at the station, as the trainmen loafed about with no idea when the all aboard could be called. It was not

wit nor entertainment those people were seeking as
they submitted an open mind to the little giant for
blow or caress. Small wonder, indeed, that the voters
were beginning to feel for political reins when they
would listen to a speech for so long.

If one did not know the name of the party flag followed by the politically Progressive lecturers of the
early nineteen hundreds, it would have been difficult
to read the design of the emblem in their platform
words. It seemed to me that they spoke in the same
tongue, and from well nigh equal conviction. Take
Joseph W. Folk, first Attorney General and then
Governor of Missouri. He was among the first to
sound the call to a new era. Or his successor in the
Governor's mansion, the able and scholarly Herbert
Hadley. Either he or the brilliant and whimsical
Henry J. Allen might easily have been nominated as
Vice President to run with Warren G. Harding in 1920,
and then, in the turn of destiny, one of them would have
found himself in the White House.

In nineteen hundred seven and eight, if one would
base his political prophecy on an appraisal of the man
and the words of his Chautauqua lecture, he would
have surely selected Warren G. Harding as a man of
the people and a champion of the rights of the greatest
number of them. But such prophesying would not
need to envision the White House ahead, to number
the prophet among the friends and admirers of the man
from Ohio. Harding was not famous then, but he was
pretty well known as a newspaperman who had been
Lieutenant Governor of his state. He was a dignified

and handsome man and a brilliant orator. He did not speak in a key greatly different from that employed by other progressive speakers, and the subject of his lecture was "The Big Stick," words of almost sacred memory. He had a virile and almost boyish enthusiasm for the organization of the circuit and for the people of the small cities. He was companionable and likeable. He liked to visit the local newspaper office, mount a stool and set a stick of type. The businessmen loved him and the crew boys almost worshipped him.

My feeling of gratitude toward Warren G. Harding was so deep that no political gossip nor scandal could ever erase it. On the Chautauqua trail he was a gentleman of sound sense and good taste. The encouragement he gave me was a sustaining strength that I needed, and I believe my colleagues of the day shared my high regard for him.

While our public were pretty broad-minded, I do not think a discussion of partisan politics would have been welcome and there was rather a firm but tacit rule against it. If it was a rule it was suspended completely, however, on two lengthy occasions. Mr. Bryan's generalship and audacity at the Baltimore Convention in 1912 projected him onto the highest planes of Chautauqua favor he had ever before occupied. The convention had continued several days longer than anyone had expected. The sessions of some of his towns were over, but we held the tents in the air until he finally arrived, and doubled up his already heavy schedule of engagements until he could catch up. We could scarcely accommodate the crowds, and the flow

of dollars into our box office was greater than ever
before or since. He had attended the Republican convention as a newspaper reporter, and people had read
so much of the excitement at Baltimore that they had
little else in mind. They all wanted to hear of the
conventions. While the matter was always put to a
vote, no one wanted "The Prince of Peace" that summer but shouted for the "Tale of Two Conventions,"
and that is what they usually got.

After the election that fall, I had some correspondence with Congressman Charles Scott of Kansas, who
chided me a bit for permitting too much discussion
from Democratic speakers and giving a lesser opportunity to the Republicans. I pointed in vain to some
of the Republicans I have named above. He thought
that was not enough and that I was inclined to choose
Democrats who were more prominent in their party
than our Republicans were in theirs. I asked him to
name some candidates from the G. O. P. whom I
might secure. He said he had never heard of Theodore
Roosevelt, for instance, or Elihu Root being engaged
on the Chautauqua. I replied that either of those two
gentlemen could name his own terms if he would con-
sent to speak. He thought it was not unlikely that he
himself might be a good addition to the program, and
even proposed a debate that suited me fine.

We finally agreed to arrange a series of joint debates
by him and Henry J. Allen of Kansas. The debates
were brilliant and exciting, and I think the two men
grew in the estimation of each other day by day. Allen
had the greater reputation as an orator, but Scott held

his own and the public derived about as much pleasure as they have ever enjoyed. So far as political comment on the outside was concerned, however, I had let myself open for plenty of criticism. The Democrats thought the Chautauqua was going Republican, and the Republicans were really mad because, since Allen was a Bull Mooser, I was accused of keeping open the breach between the two factions of the G. O. P., and apparently no politician was satisfied. The Republican Chairman of one of the states gave out a statement that the Wilson Administration was seeking to control free speech from the platform and that Horner was brought into Washington for his orders. I met up with that chairman two or three years later and told him he surely knew that his statement was far away from the facts, and he admitted the truth but thought it was pretty effective political publicity so far as he was concerned.

When I remember incidents like that and recall the honorable career of Victor Murdock and think, in retrospect, of the numerous platform celebrities who strayed a bit from the solid rock of partisanship, either heeding the call of the Bull Moose or, later, the lure of the New Deal, I am forced to think that some of them were never quite orthodox or that their adventures in the tents may have modified their views.

Since I first became old enough to take note of public matters, the people have evolved their little sarcasms and enjoyed hugely oft-repeated jokes at the expense of United States Senators. They like to think of them as a cloistered group, invested with self-created dignity, frequenting what has been termed a rich man's club. No matter though the Senator, who is fairly secure in support from his own state, is the most powerful officer in the Government, next to the President. Perhaps it is of an innate sense of equality among Americans, which generates a strange desire to raise a favorite public man to the utmost peak of public approval and then hurl a massed force to knock out all the supports while the people watch the mighty one topple to the earth. There are exceptions, of course, but it seems almost certain that if a public man can rise high enough he will often be crashed by public opinion, and about the only way he can escape is to die before the fall can overtake him. Politicians who achieve a very high place can scarcely be sure of a calm and peaceful old age, replete with the gratitude of their fellow citizens.

However, many who regarded Senators as an encrusted, aloof group, lacking human understanding and unfamiliar with the mental reactions of ordinary people, might have had some of their illusions erased, and enjoyed a jolly good time as well, if they had listened to some of my Senators of the Chautauqua Circuit.

I doubt if there was ever a more popular and generally satisfactory speaker than the Blind Statesman, from Oklahoma, Thomas Gore. Considering his affliction, no one could ever quite comprehend the deftness of his physical movements, the depths of his learning, and the adroitness of his words. As an orator, I must give him a high mark. As a silver-voiced diplomat, readying the minds of his audience for the solid blows he could strike, he had a Mark Anthonian skill. His good humor rippled like the play of water under sunlight. Though he could not see with his eyes, he had a facile talent to spread out a vista for his listeners to see. Notwithstanding the position he was said to occupy when we were facing the dread of war in 1915, I think he was more effective in advocating a strengthened American Navy even than Hobson, although the latter preceded him by several years, when the people thought even less of danger from abroad.

Another high ranker was Senator Robert Taylor, Fiddling Bob, of Tennessee. It had been said that he fiddled his way into the affections of his people although he carried no instrument on the circuit. His journey down the hot trail was lighted by the smiles of thousands. Every speech was in the white beauty of Dogwood blossoms perfumed by honeysuckles and tinkled with the songs of mockingbirds. His kindly nature beamed with the flow of fine gold. How we all loved him! May his kind live again. I joined him one day in August, 1910, at Aurora, Nebraska. The circuit was not yet very solid in finances, and no doubt there had been little rumors that things were not going too well. He asked me to take a little walk with him, as he wanted to buy some shirts, for otherwise, he said, someone would be putting him in the pest house. When he pulled out his wallet to pay for his purchase he extracted a number of familiar checks. There were some six or seven of them, each good for nine hundred dollars and they bore my signature. "I have an idea," he said, "that things are a little tough for you this summer. I have had a lot of fun, and you have been good to me. I don't need this money, and I want you to take it." I am quite sure he was very much in earnest and would have given me those thousands of dollars without regret. Needless to say, I could not accept the offered gift and I tell the story to show what kind of man he was. I have attempted to describe his lecture as a thing of rare beauty, but there was nothing tumid in it; for while it was as airy as the flight of a butterfly, it was as sound as solid metal.

When I was directing speakers for Woodrow Wilson in Chicago in 1912, I met a young man from Mississippi, then serving his first term in Congress. His name was Pat Harrison. Happily for our cause, he had already been renominated in his state and need give no thought to any campaign for election. We were the gainer because he was one of the most reliable, industrious and effective speakers on the list. I became very much attached to him and was glad to have a little part in his successful efforts to gain a seat in the Senate in 1918. His record thereafter need not be mentioned as he became one of our most sincere and constructive statesmen until he died. The brilliant Senator traveled the Premier Circuit in 1923. Oddly enough, while he was a well-defined partisan in politics, I think he was even more popular in our Republican than Democratic states. He enjoyed the tour, delivered an eloquent and persuasive lecture, and had a cordial reception, although the waters were very quiet along the political shore. The covenant of the League of Nations had been rejected by America, but we agreed that it would be well for him to make an appeal for consideration of the World Court. It was a vain effort; the people had no interest in the matter and his words fell among the rocks.

Even if the Chautauqua had engaged in the business of partisan political discussion, and could also have retained valuable factors, community accord, inspirational discourse by broad churchmen and a pretty good grade of entertainment, I think it could have produced a good model for political campaign oratory. American quadrennial campaign battles are not quite effective in furnishing a sound base for reason, logic and tolerant thought. A campaign speech is charged with passion and exaggeration and star-high pledges that must evoke misgivings even in the heart of the orator himself. Considered in relation to the utterances of the speaker's colleagues, it is as discrete as a vaudeville olio of yore, and often strays far from the straight line of truth. When the political headliner faced a Chautauqua audience he was conscious of certain platform traditions that had fostered an honest appraisal of all opinions, his own equally with those of men who did not agree with him. Therefore, Stand Pat or Progressive, Democratic or Republican, the lectures of a group of speakers using a common platform seemed to achieve an agglutinative quality that, yet, did not resist a free expression of whatever ideas these men wished to convey.

After all, it was not the political giants alone who found their names in capital letters in the Chautauqua programs. In a less news-provocative way the famous clergymen of the age were truly headliners. There were a handful of great pulpit orators who could hold their own in drawing power with the most brilliant of the statesmen. Henry Ward Beecher, one of the first of the luminaries of Redpath's list, might have looked back to the earth and beheld his mantle most creditably worn by Newell Dwight Hillis, S. Parkes Cadman and Dr. Frank W. Gunsaulus. There were three men who reached and held the heights. With all of its crudities, and there were some, the Chautauqua amply justified its march when it could enlist in service men of that heroic mold. Hillis, perhaps, moved closer to the people on the benches, and, with a lyrical quality, radiated high spirituality that struck deeply. Cadman was profound in intellectuality but quite human in his reach.

I knew Gunsaulus more intimately than the others, and I think his "Savanarola" ranks with the greatest inspirational lectures of his or any age. He was the president of the Armour Institute of Technology, and pastor of a very large People's Church. His thoughts were cast in poetry and his life moved in music. He was a master in his knowledge and appreciation of art, and his learning was as wide as the world.

I spent twelve hours with him one summer day in Estes Park in Colorado, and listened to a discourse that was twelve hours long. When we drove along the mountain stream he compared the sound of the rushing water to a symphony whose movements he analyzed. As we paused at the foot of a snow-clad peak his mind turned to geology, and he knew the scientific name of all the formations of rocks. As we returned in the early evening the wonders of astronomy found a voice in his words. The whole day was the unfolding of a heroic epode which, while it bewildered my mind, imported a strange calmness to the soul.

One Saturday at noon I telephoned his number in Chicago. His voice came back impatient and harsh. "I'm busy," it said, "I haven't time to talk; what do you want; who is it?" "This is Charles Horner," I said. "I merely called to pay my respects." "Oh," he said, "wait a minute." Then I could hear him calling to some one—"Come here"; and to me, "You stay right there—are you there?" Soon came the voices of a group of singers, and I listened to quite a concert from the study of the man who did not have time to talk. When the music was finished he asked me what I was doing. I told him I had completed my business and wanted to look at a collection of oriental rugs I had read about. He told me to wait on a certain corner. Soon he appeared, and we spent the whole afternoon looking at the specimens while I received as much of an education in history, color and design in weaving as I could absorb. I purchased a number of the beautiful things under his competent direction, and in the end he sent someone to exchange my pullman berth for a room on the train, and had the whole bundle of rugs tied together and deposited it on the train, because as the next day was to be Easter Sunday, he wanted my wife to have them without delay.

The name of Russell Conwell was known in nearly every house that possessed a Bible as well as a fireside. It is believed that his "Acres of Diamonds" was heard by more people than ever listened to any other lecture. For nearly fifty years that inspiring American classic rolled in eloquence from the pastor of Temple Church into the ears of hundreds of thousands. His tour of the Premier Circuit in 1917 was the parade of a simple, sublime and uncrowned Prince of Religion. Age and his failing health brought a mist into our eyes, but failed to dim the radiance of his words.

It would be a sorry omission to fail to record the name of Dr. George E. Vincent, the son of the great bishop who was the father of the Chautauqua.

George was president of Chautauqua Institution for several years. He was an outstanding educator, sometime President of the University of Minnesota. In the literary style and brilliance of his speaking I should classify him as among the few best of the platform. Currently, the manner and style of Adlai Steveneson, 1952 presidential candidate, most nearly resemble those of Vincent. However, the latter did not use a manuscript on the platform. Indeed, as I search my memory I cannot remember that any Chautauqua speaker I ever saw had recourse to a written address.

The men I have mentioned were not the only giants of the pulpit whose names were printed in boldface type. I cannot name them all, or indeed very many more, but I should write the names of George R. Stuart of the Southern Methodist Church, Msgr. J. Henry Tihen, onetime dean of his cathedral and later Bishop of the Catholic Church, and Dean Sumner, later Bishop of Oregon in the Episcopal Church. All in all, if political speakers had their innings, the men of the Church had their days.

Any writer who paused here and there in the Chautauqua tents over a period of more than two decades, could not close a chapter like this without a feeling of sadness. The names in Caps, the forerunner of the bright lights, may have indicated the scope but by no means measured the substance of the Chautauqua. There were other names, names that became household words. They were borne by people who were as eloquent, and, with a more rehearsed technique, became the seasoned and more comfortable heroes of the season-ticket owners. Many of them had made or have since made a good record in business or profession, apart from, but rather closely related to the platform, in law, literature, the classroom, the church, or science, or perhaps on the stage. I have already said they were too numerous to record. As I list the names of some of them, no one could know better than I the utter inadequacy of the roll, or be more conscious of the many worthy ones omitted.

I must begin with Ralph Parlette because he was the veritable shepherd of the whole Chautauqua flock. His "University of Hard Knocks," or much of it, has become a part of the language. These names are given in no order of worth or station, and are drawn from memory alone.

George D. Alden	Phil Baird
Col. George W. Bain	Bertha Kunz Baker
Elwood T. Bailey	William Sterling Battis

Lou Beauchamp
J. Adam Bede
Isabel Garhill Beecher
William Rainey Bennett
Arthur E. Bestor
Ralph Bingham
Ng. Poon Chew
William A. College
Ross Crane
D. Thomas Curtin
Smith Damron
Elias Day
John B. DeMotte
Ralph Dennis
Frank Dixon
Brooks Fletcher
Montaville Flowers
Daniel F. Fox
Glen Frank
Strickland Gillilan
Theodore Graham
Joseph Hanley
Frank Johnson
Hilton I. Jones
Sam Jones
Marcus Kavanagh
Sidney Landon
Eugene Laurant
Sylvester A. Long
Lincoln McConnell

Father McCorry
John T. McCutcheon
Bishop McDowell
Robert McIntire
Charles S. Medbury
DeWitt Miller
Adrian Newens
Edward Amherst Ott
Alton Packard
Harold Peat
Charles Plattenburg
Jess Pugh
Bishop Quayle
John B. Ratto
Opie Read
Edward Reno
Phidelah Rice
Katharine Ridgway
Frank R. Roberson
Lew Sarrett
Roy Smith
Edward A. Steiner
Z. T. Sweeney
Lorado Taft
Charles Taggart
Albert Wiggam
Herbert L. Willett
"Sunshine" Willits
Montraveille Wood

The names of most of them could be written properly with high scholastic degrees, but no collegiate honor can measure their worth. Many of them have left earthly scenes. I doubt if any of them was wealthy with much money in the bank, but they all contributed vastly to a general concept of good life and to a high realization that there is better riches than gold in the Brotherhood of Man.

It should not be thought that all of the great speakers of the Chautauqua were men. The lady platformists were quite few in number, and some of them were brilliantly successful. However, I do not think there have been a very large percentage of feminine oratorical masters, if I may borrow from the gender of the word and ascribe it to the ladies. In Chautauqua days not many women had really achieved the art of the orator. Nor do I think they have gone far yet in grasping it. Men have been working at the job for centuries and after all, women are comparatively new in public speaking. Women have always held a rank as high or even higher than their masculine contemporaries on the stage and in opera, or any sort of dramatic readings. I am duly appreciative of the talents and perfection of many modern Portias, of gentle savants and scholars and writers, and they are quite the equal of men in the art of expression.

I think there is one reason, and one only, why women have not advanced as far as they deserve in public speaking. Any one who has listened to radio broadcasting of political conventions will understand what I mean. The woman should not and need not adopt

the style and manner of her brother. Her voice has a
quality quite different from and often superior to that
of a man. Her hands have a grace of movement and
her face and body a charm which no man can possess.
She sacrifices quality, grace and charm as she adopts
the style of the male. In speaking, a man's tone range
is wider than hers. A man may raise his pitch and
amplify his tone volume for climactic emphasis. To
accomplish the same purpose she would better lower
the first but can safely add all the volume the lower
pitch can carry. Otherwise her high pitch is likely to
sound shrill. If she will use only her own physical,
mental and spiritual assets, she can easily create a feminine art in public speaking which no man can penetrate.
If I may be both bold and objective, I should say that
Ex-Congresswoman Claire Booth Luce of these new
days, furnishes a good example of a nice perfection in
speech.

However, women have achieved an equality with
men of skill in almost everything. They can even wear
trousers with distinction, and perhaps they can emulate
male oratorical methods with equal success, but I will
still insist that they had better keep their tone range
far within the confines of one octave and have some
notes to spare. In any event the mechanical amplifier
has confused, and is perhaps destroying, the art of
the spoken word as it was known in the Chautauqua.
Perhaps it is evolving a new and higher perfection, but
I think it has yet much to accomplish.

If I am hesitant to attempt a comparison of the
individual rhetorical merits of the men of the platform,

I have a positive terror of a similar effort in the case of the ladies. I am well content to offer a few examples of feminine success. High on any list must appear the name of Ruth Bryan Rhode, the daughter of the Great Commoner. She has much of the style and some of the manners in inflection and enunciation of her father. She is tall and striking in appearance and has a voice of depth and easy modulation. Her humor is sudden in essay and her words fit well in ears. She has a drawing power quite above the average and she was usually conversational in tone and companionable in style. She would delve rather deeply in a somewhat massive subject, which, however, she could keep on the line of narrative, although many of her sentences were metaphorically adorned, and were quite alive with eloquence.

Maude Ballington Booth, the Little Mother of Prisons, should always be rated as one of the most valued and useful figures of the platform. Her lecture earnings were earmarked for the service of the men who emerged from behind the bars. One can scarcely mention that great soul without a desire to write a book of a life of devotion cast on the plane of the spirit and expressed in an eloquence as sublime as her own ideals.

LaSalle Corbel Picket, wife of the Confederate General who led the brilliant charge up Cemetery Hill at Gettysburg, was a living and shining example of the grace and dignity of American womanhood. She was a beautiful creature, with white hair and flashing eyes. The people of her audience could easily imagine that they were transported into a mansion of rare beauty and taste. She possessed a regality of bearing but with a grace that was quite demure as she responded to applause with a deep curtsy that might have graced a place in the days of the Cavaliers. The grace of her presence was no less than the charm of her words, as, without bitterness or regret, she retold her stories of the Civil War.

It was from women like these and unnumbered sisters of theirs, children of music and drama, that the Chautauqua found beauty even though the setting was on a stage built of rough boards under a cloth cover that radiated heat and sometimes leaked rain. All were enriched with women of the character and type of Belle Kearney, sometime associate of Frances Willard, and Mrs. A. C. Zehner, the states lady from Texas.

Headliners or run of the mill, all Chautauqua lecturers had to have one common quality if they survived. They had to draw their lectures from their own knowledge and experience. Any excursion abroad was quickly discerned and fell flat. I once toyed with the idea of assigning a specific subject for discourse to studious and trained speakers. In laying out a program for a year or several years with the hope of embracing some educational phases, it was sometimes difficult to find the speaker to fit. Newspaper and magazine editors who wish to secure a story on a specific subject may safely commission a good writer, honest in his sense of facts, to undertake the research and produce the story. I wanted to try a similar plan for speakers. I talked to Mr. Bryan about it and he said that while he would be interested in the experiment he didn't think it would work.

I found that he was right. A writer may have his thousands of readers and if a majority of them or even some of them approve what he writes, he may be successful. His readers are not gathered together in one audience, and even his admirers have no opportunity to transmit their own sanction to fellow readers. Besides his creation may be evaluated by his written words alone. Those who listen to a lecturer may not agree with the speaker's opinions but he must win the respect of most of them if they are to say he is good. Besides they have the evidence of his appearance, his personality, and their own estimate of his veracity and sincerity to weigh with the words they hear. There is but little relation in the separate arts of the speaker and the writer, and certainly a narrower base for comparison. In short, I learned that the successful lecturer need not and should not stray far from his store of direct knowledge, nor from his own experience.

We could find young people with sparkling talent in music and for the stage. We could teach them, coach them and dress them and they would be acceptable or perhaps brilliant performers, but no one could develop a good lecturer by books or polish. With necessary talent and education, good looks and fine dress, he still had to read from the pages of the book of his own life.

FROM PEAK TO PIT

The circuit Chautauqua flourished in the spirit of unity and in the patriotic surge of the World War. It withstood the first impact of postwar boom days, and the mental and moral relaxation that attended the early twenties. The movement reached its peak in 1922 and was carried by its own momentum for more than a half dozen years longer. Some managers tried, earnestly enough, to broaden its educational base, and others were quite content to ride on the tide of popular approval. But the wisest and most devoted managers could not find much new seed to sow, nor discover a fresh fertilizer to invigorate a soil that was becoming fatigued.

It is a superficial assumption to claim that the Chautauqua was strictly an educational institution. It had good entertainment and could serve well as a sounding board for public opinion. Certainly and above all, it inspired and nourished habits of individual thinking. Not the least of its attributes was its peculiar talent to foster Community unity and action, and these in turn were its chief benefactors. The rather large number of its advocates who acclaimed the Chautauqua as a vast educational movement were reading from their own visions and not from facts. It was a good stimulus for educational processes, particularly in awakening desires to read and go to school. Some of its most enthusiastic friends exaggerated its educational virtues to such an extent that in the end the movement suffered from too much praise. As a matter of fact, its chief educational benefit was conferred upon its own personnel. We all learned more than we taught. President Harding said in 1922 that the movement had found its greatest intellectual beneficiaries among those who addressed varied audiences in differing and wide scattered communities. It offered healthful mental refreshment to the audience for a week while it furnished a graduate training school, of a kind, for its talent, crewmen, managers and agents, for a season. Aside from the benefits to its own people the Lyceum and Chautauqua had three purposes: to provide information on as many subjects as it could handle, to furnish good entertainment, and to foster the will and spirit for community unity. That it could and did use the latter to its own advantage does not reduce the value of it. Paul M. Pearson, one of its greatest leaders, said that the purpose and method of the Lyceum and Chautauqua were not to announce what people should think but to give them accurate information that would help them to think.

Many millions of people, according to our government figures, were assembling in the Chautauqua tents, and a very large number gathered in Lyceum entertainment and Lecture Halls. Managers were put to it to recruit enough of the grade of talent they must have. We could train actors, musicians and entertainers; we would produce plays and concerts and operas; but no man in good sense could produce a worth-while lecturer. Scouts had an open ear in college classrooms, listened to more sermons than they were accustomed to, penetrated Judge's Chambers and court-rooms and found front seats in conventions of all sorts. Some of them had good judgment, but others forgot that any rooster will fight better in his own barnyard.

The larger circuits with more money for talent pay suffered less than those of narrow budgets. There were not enough lecturers of weight to fill the posts. Some of us kept the best evening spots for the speakers al-though we knew well enough that a play or light opera or even a musician would attract more silver. This was not all because of idealism, but we were wise enough to know that we might thus retain the sponsorship and backing of the businessmen who signed our contracts.

One of the first causes of the decline of the Chau-tauqua was managerial inability to provide enough pow-erful speakers, and a lessening skill to promote them.

Meanwhile the entertainment features of programs were blooming and expanding. The old-time tried platform concert companies were still the most reliable, but were far too few to supply the demand. I estab-lished a producing organization and a few other man-agers took the same course. Coaches and instructors in music, platform technique and deportment were en-gaged. Composers and arrangers of scores were added to the staff, and skillful costumers were not forgotten, for we dressed our performers well. Bright, fresh and young singers and musicians were recruited from all over the land. There was no dearth of applications. If we needed a hundred new singers, for instance, perhaps as many as a thousand applicants were heard. After they were found, the difficult work remained. Many of them were untrained, or, worse, badly trained. They had to be chiseled from awkward amateurishness into some degree of professional worth. Programs of sketches, operettas and all sorts of musical vehicles had to be written. I wrote some dozens of them myself. Composers like Thurlow Lieurance or, for a time, Dr. Howard Hansen, wrote musical scores and others would make orchestrations. When we were successful in producing a company of unusual excellence there was a good market for it on other circuits, and the royalties received assisted a great deal in sustaining the organization which we called the Premier Productions. With my nose pretty close to the hearthstone, I wrote one sketch entitled "The Old Home Singers," and Thurlow Lieurance wrote the music. It was pretty much of a "Mother, home and heaven" entertainment, but the melodies were delightful. The young people in the cast were handsome, with lovely voices, and the costumes were quite elegant, in contrast to the brown canvas of the tent. It went so well that in the next few years we produced it in nearly twenty-five companies which were booked all over the United States and Canada. Scores of similar units were created; most of them were pretty good, although some fell flat and had to be taken out or reconstructed.

Wherever we went we had an eye and ear open for new and brilliant candidates for the platform, and we found them in all sorts of places. My wife and I were at dinner in our hotel in Florence, Italy, one evening, and we heard some exquisite music coming from a distant salon. It was so pleasant that I looked for the source and discovered four young people playing stringed instruments. They had a nice skill and gave the effects of a much larger organization. I found that three of them were sisters, natives of Hungary. They spoke several European languages, and we got along so well that before the evening had passed we had made contracts for the American Chautauqua Circuits. They were well received and remained in this country several years.

By way of contrast in location, I was once invited to a modest little home in Roswell, New Mexico, and was asked to listen to the music of the family—father, daughter, two sons and the daughter's husband. They turned out to be superbly simple and attractive people with evidence of native talent that no practiced ear and eye could fail to discern. I brought them to Kansas City, had them trained and coached for a few weeks, and they got along so well that they became famous in radio and stage shows. They are known as Louise Massey and her Westerners. I think no one ever knew more lovable and gentle people than they are.

Many of the young musicians of tent days went on the Broadway stage, to national broadcasting and to glittering heights in Hollywood. I would like to mention some of them, but they might be embarrassed to have anyone read of their humble start.

There was one, however, whom I can mention without fear of giving offense. He is Howard Hanson, who joined one of our little Concert Companies when he was fifteen years old. He played on the piano and cello, and, even at that age, showed that he had unusual talent. The money he earned assisted him in pursuing his studies, and perhaps his experience contributed to the nice democracy of his art. When he was several years older he toured the Premier with Glen Frank and Opie Read, the lecturers for his day. That was a company of simple and congenial greatness. Frank was a young man of brilliance and mental power. He became editor of *Century Magazine,* then president of the Wisconsin University, and later chairman of the Educational or Policy Committee of the Republican party. He was running for the Governorship of Wisconsin when he was fatally injured in an automobile accident. Opie Read, the creator of *Tennessee Judge, Starbucks,* and dozens of other novels, gave us a veritable garden of flowers in words, and had captured the symphonic beauty of the universe which he set in a rhythm of color and loveliness for our ears. He had an imagination like the sweep of a meteor, and some time in the future our grandchildren will rediscover the charm of a great poet who wrote in prose.

Hanson won a first American Scholarship of the Academy in Rome, and after he had written some symphonies that he conducted in the capitals of Europe, became the director of the Eastman School of Music and is held to be one of the greatest of American composers. Our family was very fond of him and we are happy that he wrote some of his best music in our home in Mission Hills.

Although I had ever been aware of the mastering impulse in young people to express themselves publicly in song and words, my years of work with them gave me an extended knowledge of the depth and fervor of that impulse. I was saddened by the fact that while the majority of candidates had labored diligently, and at great cost, to perfect themselves in the technique of performance, they had little or no training in the technique of projecting their talent. I had great respect and admiration for instructors in music and vocal arts in schools and private studios. There are no more diligent and conscientious people in any field of education than they were and are, but I felt that their work should be supplemented by training their students to make an acceptable public appearance.

In 1914, after a long period of planning, I established a school of music and allied activities in Kansas City, which was named the Horner Institute of Fine Arts. The policy in instruction was no different than that of other good schools. The teachers in studios and classrooms were not charged with any responsibility for the supplementary training I have indicated. That was a job for competent directors and coaches, and I cannot remember that any student or young artist was ever required to pay for it. The Institute became one that was quite unique among institutions of the kind. It earned its way to a considerable extent, or any deficit was made up with funds from our allied activities and no public appeal was ever made for money to support it. There was a surge of ambitious young people and the whole atmosphere sparkled with hope. The director of the school was a musician of note, whose unusual talent, familiarity with the aspirations of young people and broad training and experience in America and Europe, fitted him for the task to a degree better than any other man I know. He was Dr. Earl Rosenberg, and we were boyhood friends in Lexington, Nebraska.

The success and growth of the Institute were very gratifying. The student enrollment expanded to some three thousand people a year and the faculty members increased proportionately in number. We were put to it to expand our buildings and physical equipment to care for the student growth, but managed in some manner to do so. At the height of the success of the Institute, I yielded to the urging of many good friends, who were devoted to civic affairs, and gave the school, free of debt, to a group of public-spirited men. Later, when I was called to Washington for what seemed to be important duties, I resigned from the presidency of it. I must confess that the day I finally transferred the Institute was the saddest one of my life.

The use of the coaching facilities of the Institute were not restricted to our students. Perhaps not more than 5 or 10 per cent of the personnel of Chautauqua and Lyceum musical and dramatic companies were recruited from our student body. Our scouts held auditions in many places, but whether our performers came from the big or the rural places, most of them were brought to the Institute for coaching before they were committed to the circuits. Other managers seemed to like our companies because many of them commissioned us to produce some for their own circuits.

Redpath-Horner was not alone in this activity, by any means. Harry P. Harrison maintained a large and competent staff of professional directors. Ellison and White established a Conservatory of Music. Crawford Peffer and Paul Pearson were in the forefront of managers who gave great care to the preparation of their traveling companies.

I blush as I write so profusely of the activities of Redpath-Horner. My only justification is that I was more intimate with them. What I did, or sought to do, others were doing as well, or better. My consolation is that ours were typical of all the rest, and, together, combined to create a great movement which, I submit, was unique in the history of social action.

I do not state nor imply that Chautauqua people held an edge in human virtues. They were good sincere and decent folks. In standards of behavior they averaged well with the average people of the community which they served, and that was pretty good. Life was not so free and easy in those days as now. A large number of people regarded certain habits like smoking and drinking as very sinful. A majority in the Chautauqua personnel did not indulge in either, and almost universally smoking was prohibited on the Chautauqua "Ground," at least so far as our own people were concerned. It was an easy prohibition to enforce.

Some attempts to adapt programs with prevailing sentiment were funny. For instance, if the script of a play provided a dinner scene and when the lines of the hostess read "James, (the butler) serve the cocktails," no one was deceived when she said "James, serve the grapejuice." The good manager acquired enough wisdom to scan the lines in his offerings closely enough to eliminate situations or words that might provoke ridicule. Many quips were made about Chautauqua "Morality," and young performers had much sport in giggling that "We must be refined." I am positive the Chautauqua people were careful in their behavior, but in their environment it would have been difficult to be otherwise. Wrongdoing needs secret places for its performance, and there were not many such spots on this long trail.

Within a season or two the youngsters in music and entertainment learned much from old-time troupers and from the citizens of the towns with whom they associated very freely. Many a Chautauqua Concert Company grew in stature and acquired a personality as positive as that of an individual star performer.

Very often, these companies were made up of young ladies. As Vawter would have said, girls were good merchandise then, as now. Yet Vawter would have been the first to reprimand or remove a youngster who stepped out of line. Generally they were sweet, lovable and nearly always beautiful damsels. The Chautauqua trail was a golden road, and the ambition of those young performers was heart warming. The Killarney Girls, the American Girls, the Althea Players (in numerous editions), the College Singing Girls, and many, many others, brightened programs that were often heavy in content, and made joy in the tents. Yet a girl in slacks, or with bare legs or a plunging neckline or even too much make-up, might have created an

undesirable situation.   Perhaps all that was hypocrisy
in moral concept, although the Chautauqua didn't think
so at the time, and, anyhow, it was good business policy.
The fathers and mothers in the audience took the young
ladies into their homes and their hearts and most of
them longed to see their own daughters admitted into
the charmed circle of talent.

It is certain that the preachers and the church people
were the most ardent supporters of the Chautauqua.
As I have written, Sunday, for years, was the big day
in the week of entertainment.   A town that had no Sunday program would have felt hurt and cheated.   For
years many churches dismissed Sunday evening services
so that all could attend the Chautauqua.   The introduction of plays gradually produced a change of feeling.
Not that the church people did not want to see the
plays—many thousands of them witnessed their first on
the Chautauqua platform.   Yet a dramatic performance
was unseemly on a Sunday evening and not many managers dared, or desired, to offer it.   The alternative was
do two shows one day in a week, and the odd town had
to take its theatre on an afternoon.   That aroused resentment in that particular place and some of the less
religious people there took their spite out on the church
people.   That was the first split in the solid community favor.   Other people, possibly as a sort of retal-
iation, began to find fault with Sunday admission
charges.   The Sunday that had been the great friend
of old Chautauqua, became a bone of contention.
Finally, many of us came to eliminate Sunday programs

altogether, but the lost day in the week came near to
being the weight that our finances could not stand.

Our musical offerings expanded in scope and, I think,
in merit. We found we could produce an acceptable
Gilbert and Sullivan or other light opera though we
were limited in height and depth of stage. The singing
quartette grew into rather large companies as our pro-
ducers gained skill with lights, and settings. We
couldn't depend upon straight singing but adorned our
performances with some beautiful costumes and set the
whole in a good scheme of color and light with fairly
successful dramatizations of programs.

The success of the dramatic and character reader en-
couraged us to try our hand in the production of plays.
Some, like Harry Harrison and Crawford Petter, went
in for Shakespeare at first, and they engaged Ben Greet
to put together some really fine productions. My first
attempt was with *The Melting Pot,* and I secured the
aid of William Keighley as actor and director and he
showed at once, his genius for production. He was well
acquainted with the Broadway stage, and was so likable
that he could secure many of the players from original
casts of New York successes, who, I think, had their
eyes opened to the possibilities for theatrical profit far
away from the white lights of New York. One summer
Keighley captured the principal stars in a Broadway
production of *Pinafore* and from *Little Women* as
well, and we had both opera and play on one program.

The experiment was so successful that after the first
attempt in play producing, almost every Chautauqua

program included a drama of some sort and often more than one. For my part I confined our selections to proved Broadway successes, and, as the Chautauqua was regarded by New York theatre men as quite a rural affair, we could secure some of their best plays at a modest royalty, particularly as we paid for their use in a lump sum.

Keith Vawter and I secured the Chautauqua rights of *It Pays to Advertise,* and assembled a fairly complete cast of some twelve players. It was an out and out favorite, and after we were through with it it went the rounds of many other circuits, little and big, but with a diminishing cast, until at last I heard of it being played with only two or three actors.

Plays were so popular and drew so well, that when we had begun to offer them there was no way to stop. Redpath-Horner set up its own producing staff. We employed our players under "Actor's Equity" contracts, to which both management and players conformed, and we found the arrangement very satisfactory. I never had any trouble with the "Equity," nor with the "Musicians Union." Both treated me honestly and sympathetically, and were fair in fixing summer pay scales.

Keighley's manifest talent brought him into a field much more lucrative than the Chautauqua, and he became one of the foremost directors on Broadway, and, I am told, he has attained well-deserved renown in Hollywood.

Our productions, however, were modest compared to those of Crawford A. Peffer, manager of the Redpath

Circuits in New York and New England. It was he who introduced the drama to the Lyceum with a company of Ben Greet players in *The Comedy of Errors* in 1911. First and last, he sent a number of Greet groups trouping, offering various Shakespeare plays, including, *The Merchant of Venice, The Taming of the Shrew,* and *Macbeth.* Among the many plays Peffer produced a notable example was *Abraham Lincoln.* For that production Peffer went to London to arrange directly with the author, John Drinkwater. Many of Peffer's plays toured some of the more important Redpath Circuits.

Something must be written about Ben Greet. No finer, nor more sincere portrayer of Shakespearean drama ever lived. He made various trips to this country and yearned to bring Shakespeare to small cities, or any place where he could find or make a stage. He returned to England in 1914 to become the director of Old Vic theatre in London. I should speak of him as Sir Phillip Ben Greet, because he was knighted for his gallant work with the writings of the Bard of Avon. I sat backstage one evening and watched Sir Phillip at work in a very large auditorium that was not filled at all. He was doing everything, directing, working props, turning the crank of the wind machine. Costumes were at hand and sometimes he could hastily don one and reinforce the players on the stage. Even without his title he was every inch a knight. I don't think he would be offended, if he were here today, when I say he was the greatest trouper I ever saw.

Bringing the theatre to the platform had a great influence upon the Chautauqua. It was not an altogether unmixed asset. Expenses in operation were increasing, and additional receipts must be found. The play attracted many people who were strangers in the tents. On the other hand, it was plain that the ardor of sponsoring committees was diminishing. The play gave a tint of commercialism, without a doubt, and yet many thousands of customers had their first opportunity to enjoy such a thing. I think the project was not kept within reasonable bounds. It would bring the cash to the box office, but the good citizens would not strive so hard to sell season tickets. Some managers were employing directors whose experience had been limited to amateur attempts, and with tents raised in the breeze of almost every village, the quality of the drama became thin, indeed, in many places.

One of the principal causes for the decline of the movement was the vast increase in the number of Chautauquas. The businessmen of the old successful city had little heart to run booster trips throughout the county when the advertising pennants of small Chautauquas were appearing in nearly all of the villages of what they had thought was their territory. Of course the village had just as much right to have a Chautauqua as they had, and those that couldn't afford an expensive program were entitled to secure whatever they had money and population to support.

Another cause for decline was a general relaxation in concern over the discussion of public questions. The twenties brought relatively calm and placid days. Good roads were ribboning the country, and people were buying automobiles without number. Unlawful alcohol was trickling even into the dry towns whose young people had never seen a saloon. It was pleasant to dash off to a big city or to the multiplying golf courses. We had won the war and people generally were irritated to think we had had to fight it. They wanted to hear nothing of war or of our former allies whom they didn't seem to care more for than for the Germans. I imagine that if, somehow, a way could have been found for our debtor nations to pay back the money they had borrowed from us, resentment might have eased and the whole story of the days between the two wars would have been quite different.

The country suddenly found itself within the tight confines of a nationalism the like of which had not been seen before. Pulpits and platforms were resounding with complaints against Bolshevism and Socialism.

People were suspicious of foreign influences, and the eyes of all were turned to their own affairs. Prohibition and the economic plight of the farmer were about the only live issues among the people of the Midwest. A speech for the farmer would draw good applause, although too many people might adjourn to a spot behind back doors and pass around the bottle some one was always sure to produce. So far as the farmer was concerned, no one had any solace for his anxiety, balm for his wounds, nor remedy for his pocketbook, among those in or out of the Government.

The platform orators were like candidates without a platform. Few, if any, could fathom the future or logically predict any danger ahead. We had had our war and no one wanted to hear any more about it. We had had enough of reform for the present with the Federal Reserve System, Women's Votes, Direct Election of Senators, and Prohibition. Perhaps it would have been just as well to listen comfortably to New York comedies, a good band and "Mother, home and heaven" speeches, while the people groped their way out of their confused calm and indifference toward the League of Nations. The Chautauqua managers, or some of us, tried hard enough to bring some light upon that problem, as I wish to show directly, but I don't think the people were ready to regard the matter as a problem, let alone to have any light upon it. They were not at all hostile, since I never observed either heckling or hostility in any audience, but clearly the folks were apathetic.

The final and most direct blow to the Chautauqua came from the radio and talking movies. The radio was something new. Its very novelty dramatized it. Movies were of little consequence, so far as our Chautauqua life moved, until the perfection of the talkie and the comfortable embellishment of the picture theatre. Then they really cut into our crowds. As a national organization, the picture industry did not seek to injure us, but local operators in many instances were active in fermenting discord among our sponsors. They did not like to see their crowds diminish during Chautauqua week and they resented the guarantee the citizens gave us.

First of all, the plush-covered seats and the play of light and childlike simplicity of movie plot and story offered greater physical and mental ease than the Chautauqua. Not even the theatre could withstand the impact of the films. I have many good friends in the movie industry, and some of them have complimented me on the efficiency of the Chautauqua organization. Their executives are more astute than we were and permitted no obstruction in the channel leading from the box office to their cars. That is wisdom, and good both for their pocketbooks and their appraisal of popular taste, and I commend it to the sponsors of Symphony Orchestras and Grand Opera. The industry made its greatest crash in the big cities, from whence all publicity flows. Our little story of fame stemmed from the towns and small cities, and if a rural event gets into the headlines it is only for a day.

My opportunities to sense public opinion, as well as to learn something of the thoughts of political leaders, were a little better than those enjoyed by the average private citizen. My familiarity in the first gave me a certain access to the offices of the politicians. In Harding's administration, two men, and I think, only two, emerged quickly above the heads of the others. They were Charles Evans Hughes and Herbert Hoover. Even the stupidity of the Republican campaign of 1916 did not cloud the extraordinary ability of Hughes.

The calm but dramatic efficiency of Hoover as Food Administrator and as director of relief for the hungry hordes of Europe, following the war, earned warm praise from those who were informed, but he was not at all well known in America. He had never projected the story of a capable man into the news, or from public rostrums, and he would not compete with political orators who had the habit of speaking in loud tones. His friends and admirers, numerous enough, but still only a handful among millions, were strangely quiet in any song of praise. It is unfortunate for America and the world that greater use was not made of his broad knowledge of the economic and social state in a despondent Europe, but, generally, forceful leaders were scarce. To sum up, America had a sad lack of leadership, and the people were tired of being led.

For forty years the pendulum of political change had moved without rhythm and had traced its motion with seismographic significance, but there were not many eyes bright enough to read the tracings. It wrote in staccato record of movement from Cleveland to Harrison and back to Cleveland; from the placid McKinley through the vivid color of Theodore Roosevelt into the calmness of William Howard Taft. All streams, violent and unrippled, seemed to converge for a pause in the harbor of Woodrow Wilson. But the water was deep, and the dikes not strong enough to hold the tide, and the direction of the streams were confused or lost.

Wilson was a man in whom the hopes of the country merged. The sweep of his mind was wide and his understanding of humanity was warm and deep. Men had learned to build storm shelters against cyclones, to found clinics and hospitals to stay the scourge of disease, and to erect schoolhouses to cast a light into the dreary darkness of ignorance. However, they had no refuge from the earthquake of war, so that any vision remained in vision and had no substance in the public mind. War and religious impulses were the commonest occurrences in history, and only the same old tools, faith and hope, were used, rather blindly to check the one, as they advanced the other. War was thought of in terror, and men avoided thinking about it at all whenever they could. All men knew that the phenomenon of war had been inevitable thus far, but its causes were hidden behind a thick wall and it was easier to pass around than to penetrate it.

Woodrow Wilson found himself in the very front rank in leadership in a war, which, however well fought and backed with a strong will by a very patriotic people, was a conflict which our people did not want, did not understand, and resented in burning passion as soon as the flames were smothered. His Government had to stand on its war record, which was good enough, and on its plans for world peace, although there was no nice concert in the thoughts of Democratic spokesmen, some of whom were leaders who would not speak at all. We had earned a peace, and by golly we would never get into another war, so what was the use of talking about something that could not happen again. A confused and dull calm settled upon human minds, disturbed chiefly by the eddies of intolerance for anything without an American label. In such a state of public mind,

Harding was inevitable, and no other era could have produced Calvin Coolidge, whose homely wisdom and restrained speech were music in the ears.

It was not the end of war, alone, that spread the dangerous calm even while unseen and unknown economic forces were arming themselves for new conflict. If their armour had been perceived, they still were forces as little understood as the causes of war itself. The Chautauqua was important chiefly because it spoke in a coherent voice into millions of ears, and reflected more clearly than other forces the ebb and flow of public opinion. It is not strange that it lost direction since its master, public opinion, was asleep. At the height of its popularity in 1922, it made its last, and what proved to be its most futile, united effort.

There had been two great national Chautauqua and Lyceum Lecturers' Conferences, one during and one just following the war, and both had achieved success in promoting a unity in platform motive. In 1922 Paul Pearson, the president of the International Lyceum and Chautauqua Association threw himself with ardour into the job of providing a third meeting, which in attendance and range of thought was the greatest of all. He sent out a ringing call to all platform people to convene in Washington in December. It was a conference on Public Opinion and World Peace. Pearson was patient and compelling in his invitation and a large number of platform giants flocked to Washington. Their number was greatly increased by many advanced thinkers from colleges, universities and the press. Besides the unprogrammed discussions, common in such affairs, thirty-eight formal addresses were made, with spokesmen for some eighteen nations who added their weight with greater or less authority.

During that decade I made frequent trips to Europe as I had become interested in International Economics and Politics. Whatever value I gained had been aided by my enthusiasm for a new field, and particularly by a warm letter of introduction to American Diplomatic and Consular offices, written by the Secretary of State at the instance of the President. Therefore, the managing board of the Conference asked me to go to Europe in its behalf. Georges Clemenceau, the Tiger of France, War Premier, readily accepted our invitation and I was to enlist the interest of others abroad. I carried letters from Colonel E. M. House, written to various men of distinction, and I found that they were more effective in securing courteous attention to my mission than any words of commendation that anyone else could write.

I wanted most of all to persuade Lord Robert Cecil to come to the meeting. He was one of the framers of the Covenant of the League of Nations. When I called at his office in London I was informed by his secretary that his Lordship had just returned from a meeting of the League in Geneva, was quite exhausted and had retired to his home in the country, leaving word that he was not to be disturbed. I expressed my great regret and left the letter of Colonel House with the man. The next day I received a telegram from the secretary, stating that he had forwarded the letter to Lord Robert, who in turn had directed him to say that because of the importance of my introduction he would return to London and receive me the next day but one.

Lord Robert, afterwards Viscount Cecil, had presided, if my memory is accurate, at the recent Geneva meeting. His careworn appearance troubled my conscience, but he was most courteous and told me that I could stay as long as I liked and might tell him all I wanted to say. He lounged back in his leather chair, after the fashion of tall thin men, and listened without interruption. I told him of our high hopes for the Washington meeting, and of the notable speakers already secured. I said that while we had no desire to force, or even mobilize public opinion, we wanted him to present his views on the problems of world peace to our lecturers, and through them to a large section of the American population. He was warm in his praise for the project and said he would like very much to accept my invitation, but that there were certain reasons that would prevent him from doing so.

I could not escape the thought that I could surmise the chief reason why he would not come, although he did not state it definitely. His position as perhaps the foremost English advocate of the Covenant, and the views of President Harding, whose opposition was well known, might not create a pleasant situation in such a gathering. There was nothing in diplomatic niceties that should interfere, but the President, an enemy of the League, was scheduled to speak, and after all he was the Chief Executive of the nation where the meeting

was to be assembled, and Lord Roberts' participation
might not be a perfect example of good taste.

Clemenceau had no such scruples, if scruples they
were. He made one of the most forcible speeches, I
suppose, of his long career. Notwithstanding my fail-
ure in the case of Lord Robert, I had a good time on
that tour. I met some of the statesmen of Europe, including some who were, at the moment, quite prominent
in Germany. In fact the letters of Colonel House
opened all the doors I wanted to enter. No doubt my
easy American manners were a little out of form with
the more stately procedure in conversations in Europe,
and I blush a little, even yet, at one piece of informality.
I called to see Premier Venizelos of Greece. He was
not in and I was asked to leave a memorandum of the
object of my visit. I proceeded to do so with a pencil
on an ordinary writing pad, and it was casual in content as any message I might write to a close American
friend. The reply I received was couched in all the
graceful words of a state paper.

Measured by attendance figures, scope of thought,
and authoritativeness of utterances, the Conference on
Public Opinion and World Peace was as substantial
in effect as any meeting could be then. After all, President Harding did not appear but received all the dele-
gates at the White House and drew me, Paul Pearson
and Ralph Parlette, who had been his partner in a band
instrument factory, from the line to stand by his side
while the others passed to shake hands with him. I had
the privilege to preside at the first session, to make the
introductory address, and to read the message which

Mr. Harding had written. I think I should quote the letter, if for no other reason than to indicate the kind of a reputation the Chautauqua had.

The White House
Washington
December 6, 1922.

Several months ago when you first called my attention to the Lecturers' Conference of the International Lyceum and Chautauqua Association, I accepted promptly and with pleasure your invitation to attend the opening session and extend a welcome to the gathering. Since that time conditions have supervened which, involving both public duties and personal concerns, compel me to deny myself the satisfaction of appearing in person. Wherefore I am addressing you this word of regret on my own account, and of felicitation to the Association on its notable and unique effort to expand the sphere and increase the usefulness of Chautauqua.

It has been to me a personal satisfaction, as well as an intellectual and spiritual opportunity, to be numbered among the lecturers who have carried the message of Chautauqua throughout the country. Indeed one may with much confidence say that this splendid educational movement has found its greatest intellectual beneficiaries among those who, addressing varied audiences in differing and wide-scattered communities, have known the eagerness with which the people, to the number of many millions annually, seek illumination of public questions and the broadening of community vision. The time has long since passed when there could be any doubt of Chautauqua's service to the country; we are far past the era of misunderstanding when this great work could be waved aside with the light word and the gesture of tolerant superiority. Its wide appeal and high place in the public confidence have imposed upon Chautauqua an onerous responsibility, and in bringing together such a notable gathering of authorities from many lands and on many issues, to conduct here a sort of Chautauqua post-graduate course for the benefit of its lecturers, it is meeting that responsibility in a manner worthy of all approval. Chautauqua has served to reveal the individual American community to itself at its best. It has been a voluntary inspirational service in which men and women have given the best they have in them for the sake of the social interest. The conference of intellect and authority which you have brought together here suggests a certain parallel to the intellectual movements in which the universities of Europe were founded and the renaissance of learning and humanism had its beginning. It justifies, indeed, expression of the wish that this beginning might point the way toward a new advance into the light of understanding by which alone we may safely lay our course in such times as those in which we live.

Most sincerely yours,
Warren G. Harding.

I have reread, recently, some of the addresses made at that Conference, which Dr. Pearson published fully in a book. I wish everyone could read them now. I was impressed with the similarity of the views expressed then, to those we read and hear today, after the close of our greatest war. The speakers had explored the causes of political unrest and economic insecurity among the people of the world, as intelligently, and almost as thoroughly as do the thinkers now. They foresaw and feared many of the dangers that since became real and horrible. They could not find a perfect solution to the problems, or if they could, there were no means to effect it. The Chautauqua lecturers left with bulging notebooks, and a new vision of service to the world. They were at the very top of their power and affluence in engagements to speak. They had a full load of precious seed but they found barren soil.

There were no burning issues to challenge the public to expand their thought. Except for the recurring financial difficulty in agriculture, there was not much of vast national import to talk about, since all ears were closed to any sound of danger of another war. The folks had all the governmental reform they wanted, and as a matter of fact they had had too much of Government itself. No speakers I knew had enough power to rip through the dead calm and, speaking chiefly for myself, the managers had neither the imagination nor the means to plough into fresh fields.

The Chautauqua had so much momentum that it rode well for a few years longer, but I for one was losing interest in it. If it had to be content with good or bad music and entertainment as its best fruit, I had no stomach or special talent in the narrower field. Moreover, I was ready to try new things and apply whatever skill I had gained in national organization. My interest in what had been a truly real and hardy movement was waning fast. In 1926 I began to sell my circuits in pieces, and in 1928 I struck my tents for the last time. I sold the Premier in the same degree of sadness I had felt when I parted with my favorite horses in Nebraska. At the end of 1928 Mr. Rupe purchased what was left of the Premier Circuit, and I could then enjoy on summer nights the first calm sleep I had had in twenty-three years.

Other managers possessed more courage than I had, or perhaps they were not so weary. Some persisted for years. The depression of the early thirties blighted the hopes of the persistent ones. Rupe and the beloved veteran, Crawford Peffer, both continued into 1932. Rupe ceased operations in August. The last Circuit Chautauqua in the United States was the last one on the Peffer Circuit, and it closed a few days later than that at Alliance, Ohio, which was Rupe's final stand. Erickson continued his Canadian circuit as late as the summer of 1934, but finally all the big tops were sent to storage.

I am often asked if the Chautauqua will come again. I do not think so, not in the scope and character that we knew. To be sure the good Mother Chautauqua is ageless, and I think as nearly deathless as the human mind can foresee. Here and there fine assemblies of some sort are held, and will continue to function. As a national movement, effected by a confederation of many towns and cities, the Chautauqua will exist only in the memory of those who once devoted their hearts and talents to it.

I could ascribe various reasons as the basis of my opinion. The expense and difficulty of providing equipment, modern in comfort, and yet with the lure of the big tops, for instance, is one. The vast chains of commercialized entertainment is another. How can a simple home assembly compete with the charm of a magnificent spectacle on the screen with millions of dollars available for the production of it? The tremendous publicity commanded by the radio, the movies, and organized sports, could not be touched by the weak hand of country towns.

Then again, mechanical contrivances have perhaps abolished, probably modified and certainly reduced, the power of the art of public speaking. Some, maybe all, of those obstacles might be overcome. But there is another hurdle that stands like a stone wall and cannot be surmounted or penetrated unless social thinking and social philosophy are changed. In thought, practice, and quite largely in ambition, American people are urban when before they were rural. The Chautauqua was founded upon the thoughtful desire of the people of the community to improve their intellectual status. The desire was so compelling that they proceeded to effect improvement by their own joint efforts. Community life and spirit as we once knew them are receding before the white glare of centralized power and authority. That power is penetrating some sacred recesses of community ideals. It controls, very largely, our economic life, our business and our labors. Already its influence, through the mighty force of its dollars has affected our local and state governments. Surely, we must see that the outposts of the educational system which we cherished and made sacrifices for are beginning to crumple. How can we be sure that our churches, and unhappily, our freedom of thought may remain immune? There is irony for old-timers in the thought that our Government that we loudly supported and silently revered, while it is very generous, and in most respects quite sincere, is something we have come to fear. How long can fear and love go forward, hand in hand?

Thanks to a merciful God, the community still exists in some form of entity. It finds its best expression in our civic service clubs, in our local welfare organizations and in our community chests. Higher and better than all is the congregation of an American Church. That, I think, is the finest expression in American life. We should cherish those things, and encourage them to go forward hand in hand with others of their kind. It is not them, nor average Americans, nor, indeed, our government that we need fear. We should be most concerned with the apparent trend of thought that would take responsibility from our own shoulders and place it in the hands of a centralized authority, that, while conferring many blessings, is presently endangering our most priceless heritage, self-reliance.

Before dismissing the question "Will the Chautauqua come again?" with the imperfect reply I have made, one important fact should be recalled. People like to congregate on a summer evening. They like to listen to and view out-of-doors entertainment. The fine success of music festivals, like those in Hollywood, Philadelphia and in the Berkshires, illustrates the statement. The surge of summer light opera, with hundreds of thousands of listeners, in many cities offers further proof.

I hope the time may come when public-spirited citizens, in many cities, may, in the manner of the Chautauqua, combine music, the theatre, popular entertainment, with educational, scientific, religious, and other forms of discussion, into one great program of summer delight. Then the Chautauqua, as we knew it, would live again.

There is no more reason in blaming a Government for our woes than there is in placing dependence in it for our livelihood. We, the people, can control or change our authority by peaceful means, whenever we desire. I have known seven Presidents fairly well, and I have deep affection and high respect for all of them. I have known, perhaps, hundreds of our Representatives and Senators. Most of them were and are good, capable and honest men. If sometimes they erred in their acts, it is because we told them how to act or failed to tell them. Unhappily and usually, when we wrote to them it was to ask for something for ourselves, our Chamber of Commerce or for our city. Seldom have we written to them to commend them for a good deed. Now, it is for the people to decide whether we want a Government to give us things or one that will encourage us to rely more upon ourselves. We live in a wonderful and glorious land. Thousands of the products of skill and science and art are at hand for our enjoyment and to contribute to our ease and comfort. Only he who has labored through cold and hunger can best evaluate our material blessings. However, we cannot find happiness in those things. Real happiness can be found in our reliance upon God, in a life of rectitude, and in the fruits of the labor of our hands and head and heart. I do not think that it is an assumption to state that such was the chief truth that Chautauqua people tried to learn and to teach.

Chautauqua talent, managers, crewmen, teachers and all, have scattered to the four corners of the earth. Most of them are living or have lived happy and useful lives. Wherever the living ones are, I know that the comradeship of the long hot trail is a happy memory. I know that they long to clasp the hand of a fellow worker and say, "You gave a swell show."

THE END